C000039753

1,000,000 Books

are available to read at

www.ForgottenBooks.com

Read online
Download PDF
Purchase in print

ISBN 978-1-331-93722-7
PIBN 10256932

This book is a reproduction of an important historical work. Forgotten Books uses
state-of-the-art technology to digitally reconstruct the work, preserving the original format
whilst repairing imperfections present in the aged copy. In rare cases, an imperfection in
the original, such as a blemish or missing page, may be replicated in our edition. We do,
however, repair the vast majority of imperfections successfully; any imperfections that
remain are intentionally left to preserve the state of such historical works.

Forgotten Books is a registered trademark of FB &c Ltd.
Copyright © 2018 FB &c Ltd.
FB &c Ltd, Dalton House, 60 Windsor Avenue, London, SW19 2RR.
Company number 08720141. Registered in England and Wales.

For support please visit www.forgottenbooks.com

1 MONTH OF
FREE
READING

at

www.ForgottenBooks.com

By purchasing this book you are eligible for one month membership to ForgottenBooks.com, giving you unlimited access to our entire collection of over 1,000,000 titles via our web site and mobile apps.

To claim your free month visit:

www.forgottenbooks.com/free256932

* Offer is valid for 45 days from date of purchase. Terms and conditions apply.

English
Français
Deutsche
Italiano
Español
Português

www.forgottenbooks.com

Mythology Photography **Fiction**
Fishing Christianity **Art** Cooking
Essays Buddhism Freemasonry
Medicine **Biology** Music **Ancient**
Egypt Evolution Carpentry Physics
Dance Geology **Mathematics** Fitness
Shakespeare **Folklore** Yoga Marketing
Confidence Immortality Biographies
Poetry **Psychology** Witchcraft
Electronics Chemistry History **Law**
Accounting **Philosophy** Anthropology
Alchemy Drama Quantum Mechanics
Atheism Sexual Health **Ancient History**
Entrepreneurship Languages Sport
Paleontology Needlework Islam
Metaphysics Investment Archaeology
Parenting Statistics Criminology
Motivational

BLACKIE'S ENGLISH SCHOOL TEXTS

EDITED BY W. H. D. ROUSE, LITT.D.

The
Taking of the Galleon

From Lord Anson's Voyage

BLACKIE & SON LIMITED 50 OLD BAILEY

LONDON E.C. GLASGOW AND DUBLIN 1905

BLACKIE'S
ENGLISH SCHOOL TEXTS

EDITED BY

W. H. D. ROUSE, Litt.D.
Head-master of the Perse School, Cambridge

In cloth covers, price Sixpence each

Defoe's Journal of the Plague Year
Washington Irving's Companions of Columbus
Sir Richard Hawkins's Voyage into the South Seas
Tales from the Decameron
Erasmus's Praise of Folly
Macaulay's First Chapter
Macaulay's Second Chapter
Dickens's Christmas Carol
Lamb's Schooldays and other Essays
North's Plutarch: Alexander the Great
Stories of Antonio and Benedict Mol, from Borrow's
    Bible in Spain
Gipsy Stories, from Borrow's Bible in Spain
Napier's Great Battles of the Peninsular War (Two
    Volumes)
Hawthorne's Tanglewood Tales
The Story of Sindbad (Lane's Arabian Nights)
Raleigh's Discovery of Guiana
Drake's World Encompassed
Robinson Crusoe
Washington Irving's Rip van Winkle
Purchas his Pilgrimes—Early Voyages to Japan
Kingsley's Heroes
Gulliver's Travels
Lamb's Adventures of Ulysses
Tales from the Arabian Nights
Trips to Wonderland, from Lucian.
The Taking of the Galleon
The Embassy to the Great Mogul
Sojourn at Lhassa
Others to follow

DA
87
.1
A6A2
1905
JAN 18 1966
1041213

INTRODUCTION

GEORGE ANSON was born in the year 1697, and used the sea from his boyhood. He saw service at the age of fifteen, and served under Sir John Norris in the Baltic and the North Sea. In 1724 he was in command of a frigate protecting commerce off the coast of North America; here and in the West Indies and Africa he served in the same capacity against the French for several years. In 1740 he commanded a squadron in the Pacific, and inflicted great loss on the Spaniards: at this time comes his famous voyage round the world, which ended in 1744, when he returned home with rich prizes. As Vice-Admiral of the Channel Fleet, he defeated the French off Cape Finisterre in 1747, when he was created Baron Anson. He was First Lord of the Admiralty for two periods of five years each, and died in 1762 as Admiral of the Fleet.

This volume contains one of the best episodes of his voyage round the world, the long pursuit of the Spanish treasure ship ending in its capture.

THE TAKING OF THE GALLEON

CHAPTER I

The run from the coast of Mexico to the Ladrones or Marian islands.

WHEN, on the 6th of May 1742, we left the coast of America, we stood to the S.W. with a view of meeting with the N.E. trade-wind, which the accounts of former writers made us expect at seventy or eighty leagues' distance from the land : we had, besides, another reason for standing to the southward, which was the getting into the latitude of 13° or 14° north ; that being the parallel where the Pacific Ocean is most usually crossed, and consequently where the navigation is esteemed the safest : this last purpose we had soon answered, being in a day or two sufficiently advanced to the south. At the same time we were also farther from the shore than we had presumed was necessary for the falling in with the trade-wind : but in this particular we were most grievously disappointed ; for the wind still continued to the west-ward, or at best variable. As the getting into the N.E. trade was to us a matter of the last consequence, we

5

stood more to the southward, and made many experiments to meet with it; but all our efforts were for a long time unsuccessful: so that it was seven weeks, from our leaving the coast, before we got into the true trade-wind. This was an interval in which we believed we should well-nigh have reached the easternmost parts of Asia: but we were so baffled with the contrary and variable winds, which for all that time perplexed us, that we were not as yet advanced above a fourth part of the way. The delay alone would have been a sufficient mortification; but there were other circumstances attending it, which rendered this situation not less terrible, and our apprehensions perhaps still greater than in any of our past distresses. For our two ships were by this time extremely crazy; and many days had not passed before we discovered a spring in the foremast of the Centurion, which rounded about twenty-six inches of its circumference, and which was judged to be at least four inches deep: and no sooner had our carpenters secured this with fishing it, but the Gloucester made a signal of distress; and we learnt that she had a dangerous spring in her mainmast, twelve feet below the trussel-trees; so that she could not carry any sail upon it. Our carpenters, on a strict examination of this mast, found it so very rotten and decayed, that they judged it necessary to cut it down as low as it appeared to have been injured; and by this it was reduced to nothing but a stump, which served only as a step to the topmast. These accidents augmented our delay, and occasioned us great anxiety about our future security: for, on our leaving the coast of Mexico, the scurvy had begun to make its appearance again amongst our people; though from our departure from Juan Fernandes we had till then enjoyed a most uninterrupted state of health. We too well knew the effects of this disease, from our former fatal experience, to suppose that anything but a speedy passage could secure the greater part of our crew from perishing by it: and as, after being seven weeks at sea, there did not appear any reasons that could persuade us we were nearer the trade-wind than when we first set out, there was no ground for us to suppose but our passage would prove at least three times as long as we at first expected; and consequently we had the melancholy prospect, either of dying by the scurvy, or perishing with the ship for want of hands to navigate her.

I have already observed that, a few days after our running off the coast of Mexico, the Gloucester had her mainmast cut down to a stump, and we were obliged to fish our foremast; and that these misfortunes were greatly aggravated by our meeting with contrary and variable winds for near seven weeks. I shall now add that when we reached the trade-wind, and it settled between the north and the east, yet it seldom blew with so much strength, but the Centurion might have carried all her small sails abroad with the greatest safety; so that now, had we been a single ship, we might have run down our longitude apace, and have reached the Ladrones soon enough to have recovered great numbers of our men, who afterwards perished. But the Gloucester, by the loss of her mainmast, sailed so very heavily, that we had seldom any more than our topsails set, and yet were frequently obliged to lie-to for her: and, I conceive, that in the whole we lost little less than a month by our attendance upon her, in consequence of the various mischances she encountered. In all this run it was remarkable that we were rarely many days together without seeing great numbers of birds; which is a proof that there are many islands, or at least rocks, scattered all along at no very considerable distance from our track. Some, indeed, there are marked in the Spanish chart, hereafter mentioned; but the frequency of the birds seem to evince that there are many more than have been hitherto discovered; for the greatest part of the birds we observed were such as are known to roost on shore; and the manner of their appearance sufficiently made out that they came from some distant haunt every morning, and returned thither again in the evening; for we never saw them early or late; and the hour of their arrival and departure gradually varied, which we supposed was occasioned by our running nearer their haunts or getting further from them.

The trade-wind continued to favour us without any fluctuation, from the end of June till towards the end of July. But on the 26th of July, being then, as we esteemed, about three hundred leagues distant from the Ladrones, we met with a westerly wind, which did not come about again to the eastward in four days' time. This was a most dispiriting incident, as it at once damped all our hopes of speedy relief, especially too as it was attended with a vexatious accident to the Gloucester: for in one part of these four days the wind flattened to a calm, and the ships rolled very deep; by which means the Gloucester's forecap split, and her top-mast came by the board, and broke her foreyard directly in the slings. As she was hereby rendered incapable of making any sail for some time, we were obliged, as soon as the gale sprang up, to take her in tow; and near twenty of the healthiest and ablest of our seamen were taken from the business of our own ship, and were employed for eight or ten days together on board the Gloucester in repairing her damages: but these things, mortifying as we thought them, were but the beginning of our disasters; for scarce had our people finished their business in the Gloucester, before we met with a most violent storm in the western board, which obliged us to lie-to. In the beginning of this storm our ship sprang a leak and let in so much water that all our people, officers included, were employed continually in working the pumps: and the next day we had the vexation to see the Gloucester, with her top-mast once more by the board; and whilst we were viewing her with great concern for this new distress, we saw her main-topmast, which had hitherto served as a jury mainmast, share the same fate. This completed our misfortunes, and rendered them without resource; for we knew the Gloucester's crew were so few and feeble, that without our assistance they could not be relieved: and our sick were now so far increased, and those that remained in health so continually fatigued with the additional duty of our pumps, that it was impossible for us to lend them any aid. Indeed we were not as yet fully apprised of the deplorable situation of the Gloucester's crew; for when the storm abated (which during its continuance prevented all communication with them), the Gloucester bore up under our stern; and Captain Mitchel informed the commodore that besides the loss of his masts, which was all that had appeared to us, the ship had then no less than seven feet of water in her hold, although his officers and men had been kept constantly at the pumps for the last twenty-four hours.

This last circumstance was indeed a most terrible accumulation to the other extraordinary distresses of the Gloucester, and required, if possible, the most speedy and vigorous assistance; which Captain Mitchel begged the commodore to send him: but the debility of our people, and our own immediate preservation, rendered it impossible for the commodore to comply with his request. All that could be done was to send our boat on board for a more particular condition of the ship; and it was soon suspected that the taking her people on board us, and then destroying her, was the only measure that could be prosecuted in the present emergency, both for the security of their lives and of our own.

Our boat soon returned with a representation of the state of the Gloucester, and of her several defects, signed by Captain Mitchel and all his officers; by which it appeared that she had sprung a leak by the stern-post being loose, and working with every roll of the ship, and by two beams a-midships being broken in the orlop; no part of which the carpenters reported was possible to be repaired at sea: that both officers and men had worked twenty-four hours at the pumps without intermission, and were at length so fatigued that they could continue their labour no longer, but had been forced to desist, with seven feet of water in the hold, which covered their casks, so that they could neither come at fresh water, nor provision: that they had no mast standing, except the foremast, the mizen-

mast, and the mizen-topmast, nor had they any spare
masts to get up in the room of those they had lost: that
the ship was besides extremely decayed in every part,
for her knees and clamps were all worked quite loose,
and her upper works in general were so loose that the
quarter-deck was ready to drop down: and that her
crew was greatly reduced, for there remained alive on
board her no more than seventy-seven men, eighteen
boys, and two prisoners, officers included; and that of
this whole number only sixteen men and eleven boys
were capable of keeping the deck, and several of these
very infirm.

The commodore, on the perusal of this melancholy
representation, presently ordered them a supply of water
and provisions, of which they seemed to be in immediate
want, and at the same time sent his own carpenter on
board them to examine into the truth of every particular;
and it being found, on the strictest inquiry, that the
preceding account was in no instance exaggerated, it
plainly appeared that there was no possibility of preserving the Gloucester any longer, as her leaks were
irreparable, and the united hands on board both ships,
capable of working, would not be able to free her, even
if our own ship should not employ any part of them.
What then could be resolved on, when it was the utmost
we ourselves could do to manage our own pumps?
indeed there was no room for deliberation; the only
step to be taken was the saving the lives of the few
that remained on board the Gloucester, and getting
out of her as much as possible before she was destroyed.
And therefore the commodore immediately sent an
order to Captain Mitchel, as the weather was now

calm and favourable, to send his people on board the Centurion as expeditiously as he could; and to take out such stores as he could get at, whilst the ship could be kept above water. And as our leak required less attention, whilst the present easy weather continued, we sent our boats with as many men as we could spare, to Captain Mitchel's assistance.

The removing the Gloucester's people on board us, and the getting out such stores as could most easily be come at, gave us full employment for two days. Mr. Anson was extremely desirous to have gotten two of her cables and an anchor, but the ship rolled so much, and the men were so excessively fatigued, that they were incapable of effecting it; nay, it was even with the greatest difficulty that the prize-money, which the Gloucester had taken in the South Seas, was secured, and sent on board the Centurion: however, the prize-goods on board her, which amounted to several thousand pounds in value, and were principally the Centurion's property, were entirely lost; nor could any more provision be got out than five casks of flour, three of which were spoiled by the salt water. Their sick men, amounting to near seventy, were removed into boats with as much care as the circumstances of that time would permit; but three or four of them expired as they were hoisting them into the Centurion.

It was the 15th of August, in the evening, before the Gloucester was cleared of everything that was proposed to be removed; and though the hold was now almost full of water, yet as the carpenters were of opinion that she might still swim for some time if the calm should continue, and the water become smooth, she was set on fire; for we knew not how near we might now be to the island of Guam, which was in the possession of our enemies, and the wreck of such a ship would have been to them no contemptible acquisition. When she was set on fire, Captain Mitchel and his officers left her, and came on board the Centurion: and we immediately stood from the wreck, not without some apprehensions (as we had now only a light breeze) that if she blew up soon, the concussion of the air might damage our rigging; but she fortunately burnt, though very fiercely, the whole night, her guns firing successively as the flames reached them. And it was six in the morning, when we were about four leagues distant, before she blew up; the report she made upon this occasion was but a small one, but there was an exceeding black pillar of smoke, which shot up into the air to a very considerable height.

Thus perished His Majesty's ship the Gloucester. And now it might have been expected, that being freed from the embarrassments which her frequent disasters had involved us in, we might proceed on our way much brisker than we had hitherto done, especially as we had received some small addition to our strength, by the taking on board the Gloucester's crew; but our anxieties were not yet to be relieved; for, notwithstanding all that we had hitherto suffered, there remained much greater distresses, which we were still to struggle with. For the late storm, which had proved so fatal to the Gloucester, had driven us to the northward of our intended course; and the current setting the same way, after the weather abated, had forced us still a degree or two farther, so that we were now in $17\frac{1}{4}°$ of North latitude, instead of being in $13\frac{1}{2}°$, which was the parallel we proposed to

keep, in order to reach the island of Guam: and as it
had been a perfect calm for some days since the cessation of the storm, and we were ignorant how near we
were to the meridian of the Ladrones, and supposed
ourselves not to be far from it, we apprehended that we
might be driven to the leeward of them by the current,
without discovering them: in this case, the only land
we could make would be some of the eastern parts of
Asia, where, if we could arrive, we should find the
western monsoon in its full force, so that it would be
impossible for the stoutest best-manned ship to get in.
And this coast being removed between four and five
hundred leagues farther, we, in our languishing circumstances, could expect no other than to be destroyed by
the scurvy long before the most favourable gale could
carry us to such a distance: for our deaths were now
extremely alarming, no day passing in which we did
not bury eight or ten, and sometimes twelve, of our
men; and those who had hitherto continued healthy
began to fall down apace. Indeed we made the best
use we could of the present calm, by employing our
carpenters in searching after the leak, which was now
considerable, notwithstanding the little wind we had: the
carpenters at length discovered it to be in the gunner's
fore-storeroom, where the water rushed in under the
breast-hook, on each side of the stem; but though they
found where it was, they agreed that it was impossible
to stop it till we should get into port, and till they
could come at it on the outside; however, they did the
best they could within-board, and were fortunate enough
to reduce it, which was a considerable relief to us.

We had hitherto considered the calm which succeeded

the storm, and which continued for some days, as a very
great misfortune; since the currents were driving us to
the northward of our parallel, and we thereby risked the
missing of the Ladrones, which we now conceived ourselves to be very near. But when a gale sprang up, our
condition was still worse; for it blew from the S.W.,
and consequently was directly opposed to the course we
wanted to steer: and though it soon veered to the N.E.,
yet this served only to tantalise us, for it returned back
again in a very short time to its old quarter. However,
on the 22nd of August we had the satisfaction to find
that the current was shifted, and had set us to the
southward: and the 23rd, at daybreak, we were cheered
with the discovery of two islands in the western board:
this gave us all great joy, and raised our drooping spirits;
for before this a universal dejection had seized us, and
we almost despaired of ever seeing land again: the
nearest of these islands we afterwards found to be
Anatacan; we judged it to be full fifteen leagues from
us, and it seemed to be high land, though of an indifferent length: the other was the island of Serigan; and
had rather the appearance of a high rock than a place
we could hope to anchor at. We were extremely impatient to get in with the nearest island, where we
expected to meet with anchoring-ground, and an opportunity of refreshing our sick: but the wind proved so
variable all day, and there was so little of it, that we
advanced towards it but slowly; however, by the next
morning we were got so far to the westward that we were
in view of a third island, which was that of Paxaros,
though marked in the chart only as a rock. This was
small and very low land, and we had passed within less

than a mile of it in the night without seeing it: and now at noon, being within four miles of the island of Anatacan, the boat was sent away to examine the anchoring-ground and the produce of the place; and we were not a little solicitous for her return, as we then conceived our fate to depend upon the report we should receive: for the other two islands were obviously enough incapable of furnishing us with any assistance, and we knew not then that there were any others which we could reach. In the evening the boat came back, and the crew informed us that there was no place for a ship to anchor, the bottom being everywhere foul ground, and all, except one small spot, not less than fifty fathoms in depth; that on that spot there was thirty fathoms, though not above half-a-mile from the shore; and that the bank was steep too, and could not be depended on: they further told us that they had landed on the island, but with some difficulty, on account of the greatness of the swell; that they found the ground was everywhere covered with a kind of wild cane, or rush; but that they met with no water, and did not believe the place to be inhabited; though the soil was good, and abounded with groves of cocoa-nut trees.

This account of the impossibility of anchoring at this island occasioned a general melancholy on board; for we considered it as little less than the prelude to our destruction; and our despondency was increased by a disappointment we met with the succeeding night; for, as we were plying under topsails, with an intention of getting nearer to the island, and of sending our boat on shore to load with cocoa-nuts for the refreshment of our sick, the wind proved squally, and blew so strong off shore, that we were driven so far to the southward, that we dared not send off our boat. And now the only possible circumstance, that could secure the few which remained alive from perishing, was the accidental falling in with some other of the Ladrone Islands better prepared for our accommodation; and as our knowledge of these islands was extremely imperfect, we were to trust entirely to chance for our guidance; only as they are all of them usually laid down near the same meridian, and we had conceived those we had already seen to be part of them, we concluded to stand to the southward as the most probable means of falling in with the next. Thus, with the most gloomy persuasion of our approaching destruction, we stood from the island of Anatacan, having all of us the strongest apprehensions (and those not ill founded) either of dying of the scurvy, or of perishing with the ship, which, for want of hands to work her pumps, might in a short time be expected to founder.

CHAPTER II

Our arrival at Tinian, and an account of the island, and
  of our proceedings there, till the Centurion drove out
  to sea.

It was on the 26th of August 1742, in the morning,
when we lost sight of Anatacan. The next morning we
discovered three other islands to the eastward, which
were from ten to fourteen leagues from us. These were,
as we afterwards learnt, the islands of Saypan, Tinian,
and Aguigan. We immediately steered towards Tinian,
which was the middlemost of the three, but had so much
of calms and light airs, that though we were helped
forwards by the currents, yet next day, at daybreak, we
were at least five leagues distant from it. However, we
kept on our course, and about ten in the morning we
perceived a proa under sail to the southward, between
Tinian and Aguigan. As we imagined from hence that
these islands were inhabited, and knew that the Spaniards
had always a force at Guam, we took the necessary precautions for our own security, and for preventing the
enemy from taking advantage of our present wretched
circumstances, of which they would be sufficiently informed by the manner of our working the ship; we

18

therefore mustered all our hands, who were capable of
standing to their arms, and loaded our upper and quarter-
deck guns with grape-shot; and that we might the more
readily procure some intelligence of the state of these
islands, we showed Spanish colours, and hoisted a red
flag at the fore topmast-head, to give our ship the appearance of the Manila galleon, hoping thereby to decoy
some of the inhabitants on board us. Thus preparing
ourselves, and standing towards the land, we were near
enough, at three in the afternoon, to send the cutter in
shore to find out a proper berth for the ship; and we
soon perceived that a proa came off the shore to meet
the cutter, fully persuaded, as we afterwards found, that
we were the Manila ship. As we saw the cutter returning back with the proa in tow, we immediately sent the
pinnace to receive the proa and the prisoners, and to
bring them on board, that the cutter might proceed on
her errand. The pinnace came back with a Spaniard
and four Indians, which were the people taken in the
proa. The Spaniard was immediately examined as to
the produce and circumstances of this island of Tinian,
and his account of it surpassed even our most sanguine
hopes; for he informed us that it was uninhabited,
which, in our present defenceless condition, was an
advantage not to be despised, especially as it wanted
but few of the conveniences that could be expected in
the most cultivated country; for he assured us that
there was great plenty of very good water, and that
there were an incredible number of cattle, hogs, and
poultry running wild on the island, all of them excellent
in their kind; that the woods produced sweet and sour
oranges, limes, lemons, and cocoa-nuts in great plenty,

besides a fruit peculiar to these islands (called by
Dampier, bread-fruit); that from the quantity and good-
ness of the provisions produced here, the Spaniards at
Guam made use of it as a store for supplying the garrison;
that he himself was a sergeant of that garrison, and was
sent there with twenty-two Indians to jerk beef, which
he was to load for Guam on board a small bark of about
fifteen tons, which lay at anchor near the shore.

This account was received by us with inexpressible
joy: part of it we were ourselves able to verify on the
spot, as we were by this time near enough to discover
several numerous herds of cattle feeding in different
places of the island; and we did not any ways doubt
the rest of his relation, as the appearance of the shore
prejudiced us greatly in its favour, and made us hope,
that not only our necessities might be there fully relieved, and our diseased recovered, but that, amidst
those pleasing scenes which were then in view, we might
procure ourselves some amusement and relaxation after
the numerous fatigues we had undergone: for the
prospect of the country did by no means resemble that
of an uninhabited and uncultivated place, but had much
more the air of a magnificent plantation, where large
lawns and stately woods had been laid out together with
great skill, and where the whole had been so artfully
combined, and so judiciously adapted to the slopes of
the hills, and the inequalities of the ground, as to produce a most striking effect, and to do honour to the
invention of the contriver. Thus (an event not unlike
what we had already seen) we were forced upon the
most desirable and salutary measures by accidents, which
at first sight we considered as the greatest of misfortunes;

for had we not been driven by the contrary winds and currents to the northward of our course (a circumstance, which at that time gave us the most terrible apprehensions), we should, in all probability, never have arrived at this delightful island, and consequently we should have missed of that place, where alone all our wants could be most amply relieved, our sick recovered, and our enfeebled crew once more refreshed, and enabled to put again to sea.

The Spanish sergeant, from whom we received the account of the island, having informed us that there were some Indians on shore under his command, employed in jerking beef, and that there was a barque at anchor to take it on board, we were desirous, if possible, to prevent the Indians from escaping, who, doubtless, would have given the governor of Guam intelligence of our arrival; and we therefore immediately dispatched the pinnace to secure the barque, which the sergeant told us was the only embarkation on the place; and then, about eight in the evening, we let go our anchor in twenty-two fathoms; and though it was almost calm, and whatever vigour and spirit was to be found on board was doubtless exerted to the utmost on this pleasing occasion, when, after having kept the sea for some months, we were going to take possession of this little paradise, yet we were full five hours in furling our sails: it is true, we were somewhat weakened by the crews of the cutter and pinnace, which were sent on shore; but it is not less true, that, including those absent with the boats and some negro and Indian prisoners, all the hands we could muster capable of standing at a gun amounted to no more than seventy-one, most of which number,

too, were incapable of duty; but on the greatest
emergencies this was all the force we could collect, in
our present enfeebled condition, from the. united crews
of the Centurion, the Gloucester, and the Tryal, which,
when we departed from England, consisted altogether of
near a thousand hands.

When we had furled our sails, the remaining part of
the night was allowed to our people for their repose, to
recover them from the fatigue they had undergone; and
in the morning a party was sent on shore, well armed,
of which I myself was one, to make ourselves masters of
the landing-place, as we were not certain what opposition
might be made by the Indians on the Island: we landed
without difficulty, for the Indians having perceived, by
our seizure of the barque the night before, that we were
enemies, they immediately fled into the woody parts of
the island. We found on shore many huts which they
had inhabited, and which saved us both the time and
trouble of erecting tents; one of these huts which the
Indians made use of for a storehouse was very large,
being twenty yards long and fifteen broad; this we
immediately cleared of some bales of jerked beef, which
we found in it, and converted it into an hospital for our
sick, who, as soon as the place was ready to receive
them, were brought on shore, being in all a hundred and
twenty-eight: numbers of these were so very helpless,
that we were obliged to carry them from the boats to
the hospital upon our shoulders, in which humane
employment (as before at Juan Fernandes) the commodore himself, and every one of his officers, were
engaged without distinction; and, notwithstanding the
great debility and the dying aspects of the greatest part

of our sick, it is almost incredible how soon they began to feel the salutary influence of the land; for, though we buried twenty-one men on this and the preceding day, yet we did not lose above ten men more during our whole two months' stay here; and in general, our diseased received so much benefit from the fruits of the island, particularly the fruits of the acid kind, that, in a week's time, there were but few who were not so far recovered as to be able to move about without help.

And now being in some sort established at this place, we were enabled more particularly to examine its qualities and productions; and that the reader may the better judge of our manner of life here, and future navigators be better apprised of the conveniences we met with, I shall, before I proceed any further in the history of our own adventures, throw together the most interesting particulars that came to our knowledge, in relation to the situation, soil, produce, and conveniences of this island of Tinian.

This island lies in the latitude of 15° 8' north, and longitude from Acapulco 114° 50' west. Its length is about twelve miles, and its breadth about half as much; it extending from the S.S.W. to N.N.E. The soil is everywhere dry and healthy, and somewhat sandy, which, being less disposed than other soils to a rank and over luxuriant vegetation, occasions the meadows and the bottoms of the woods to be much neater and smoother than is customary in hot climates. The land rises by easy slope from the very beach where we watered to the middle of the island; though the general course of its ascent is often interrupted and traversed by gentle descents and valleys; and the inequalities that are formed by the different combinations of these gradual swellings of the ground are most beautifully diversified with large lawns, which are covered with a very fine trefoil, intermixed with a variety of flowers, and are skirted by woods of tall and well-spread trees, most of them celebrated either for their aspect or their fruit. The turf of the lawns is quite clean and even, and the bottoms of the woods in many places clear of all bushes and underwoods; and the woods themselves usually terminate on the lawns with a regular outline, not broken, nor confused with straggling trees, but appearing as uniform as if laid out by art. Hence arose a great variety of the most elegant and entertaining prospects, formed by the mixture of these woods and lawns, and their various intersections with each other, as they spread themselves differently through the valleys and over the slopes and declivities with which the place abounds. The fortunate animals, too, which for the greatest part of the year are the sole lords of this happy soil, partake in some measure of the romantic cast of the island, and are no small addition to its wonderful scenery: for the cattle, of which it is not uncommon to see herds of some thousands feeding together in a large meadow, are certainly the most remarkable in the world; for they are all of them milk-white, except their ears, which are generally black. And though there are no inhabitants here, yet the clamour and frequent parading of domestic poultry, which range the woods in great numbers, perpetually excite the ideas of the neighbourhood of farms and villages, and greatly contribute to the cheerfulness and beauty of the place. The cattle on the island we computed were at least ten thousand; and we had no difficulty in getting near them, as they were not shy of us. Our first method of killing them was shooting them; but at last, when, by accidents to be hereafter recited, we were obliged to husband our ammunition, our men ran them down with ease. Their flesh was extremely well tasted, and was believed by us to be much more easily digested than any we had ever met with. The fowls too were exceeding good, and were likewise run down with little trouble; for they could scarcely fly farther than a hundred yards at a flight, and even that fatigued them so much that they could not readily rise again; so that, aided by the openness of the woods, we could at all times furnish ourselves with whatever number we wanted. Besides the cattle and the poultry, we found here abundance of wild hogs: these were most excellent food; but as they were a very fierce animal, we were obliged either to shoot them, or to hunt them with large dogs, which we found upon the place at our landing, and which belonged to the detachment which was then upon the island amassing provisions for the garrison of Guam. As these dogs had been purposely trained to the killing of the wild hogs, they followed us very readily, and hunted for us; but though they were a large bold breed, the hogs fought with so much fury that they frequently destroyed them, so that we by degrees lost the greatest part of them.

But this place was not only extremely grateful to us from the plenty and excellence of its fresh provisions, but was as much perhaps to be admired for its fruits and vegetable productions, which were most fortunately adapted to the cure of the sea scurvy, which had so terribly reduced us. For in the woods there were inconceivable quantities of cocoa-nuts, with the cabbages growing on the same tree: there were besides guavoes, limes, sweet and sour oranges, and a kind of fruit, peculiar to these islands, called by the Indians, rima, but by us the bread-fruit, for it was constantly eaten by us during our stay upon the island instead of bread, and so universally preferred to it, that no ship's bread was expended during that whole interval. It grew upon a tree which is somewhat lofty, and which, towards the top, divides into large and spreading branches. The leaves of this tree are of a remarkable deep green, are notched about the edges, and are generally from a foot to eighteen inches in length. The fruit itself grows indifferently on all parts of the branches; it is in shape rather elliptical than round, is covered with a rough rind, and is usually seven or eight inches long; each of them grows singly and not in clusters. This fruit is fittest to be used when it is full grown, but is still green; in which state its taste has some distant resemblance to that of an artichoke bottom, and its texture is not very different; for it is soft and spongy. As it ripens it grows softer and of a yellow colour, and then contracts a luscious taste, and an agreeable smell, not unlike a ripe peach; but then it is esteemed unwholesome, and is said to produce fluxes. Besides the fruits already enumerated, there were many other vegetables extremely conducive to the cure of the malady we had long laboured under, such as water-melons, dandelion, creeping purslain, mint, scurvy-grass, and sorrel; all which, together with the fresh meats of the place, we devoured with great eagerness, prompted thereto by the strong inclination which nature never fails of exciting in scorbutic disorders for these powerful specifics.

It will easily be conceived from what hath been already said, that our cheer upon this island was in some degree luxurious, but I have not yet recited all the varieties of provision which we here indulged in. Indeed we thought it prudent totally to abstain from fish, the few we caught at our first arrival having surfeited those who ate of them; but considering how much we had been inured to that species of food, we did not regard this circumstance as a disadvantage, especially as the defect was so amply supplied by the beef, pork, and fowls already mentioned, and by great plenty of wild fowl; for I must observe, that near the centre of the island there were two considerable pieces of fresh water, which abounded with duck, teal, and curlew: not to mention the whistling plover, which we found there in prodigious plenty.

In this place the Centurion anchored in twenty and twenty-two fathom water, opposite to a sandy bay, and about a mile and a half distant from the shore. The bottom of this road is full of sharp-pointed coral rocks, which, during four months of the year, that is, from the middle of June to the middle of October, renders it a very unsafe place to lie at. This is the season of the western monsoons, when near the full and change of the moon, but more particularly at the change, the wind is usually variable all round the compass, and seldom fails to blow with such fury that the stoutest cables are not to be confided in. What adds to the danger at these times is the excessive rapidity of the tide of flood, which sets to the S.E. between this island and that of Aguiguan, a small island near the southern extremity of Tinian. This tide runs at first with a vast head and overfall of water, and occasions such a hollow and overgrown sea as is scarcely to be conceived; so that (as will be hereafter more particularly mentioned) we were under the dreadful apprehension of being pooped by it, though we were in a sixty-gun ship. In the remaining eight months of the year, that is, from the middle of October to the middle of June, there is a constant season of settled weather, when, if the cables are but well armed, there is scarcely any danger of their being so much as rubbed; so that during all that interval it is as secure a road as could be wished for. I shall only add that the anchoring bank is very shelving, and stretches along the S.W. end of the island, and that it is entirely free from shoals, except a reef of rocks which is visible and lies about half-a-mile from the shore, and affords a narrow passage into a small sandy bay, which is the only place where boats can possibly land. After this account of the island and its produce, it is necessary to return to our own history.

Our first undertaking after our arrival was the removal of our sick on shore, as hath been mentioned. Whilst we were thus employed, four of the Indians on shore, being part of the Spanish sergeant's detachment, came and surrendered themselves to us, so that with those we took in the proa we had now eight of them in our custody. One of the four who submitted undertook to show us the most convenient place for killing cattle, and two of our men were ordered to attend him on that service; but one of them unwarily trusting the Indian with his firelock and pistol, the Indian escaped with them into the woods: his countrymen who remained behind were apprehensive of suffering for this perfidy of their comrade, and therefore begged leave to send one of their own party into the country, who they engaged should both bring back the arms and persuade the whole detachment from Guam to submit to us. The commodore granted their request, and one of them was despatched on this errand, who returned next day and brought back the firelock and pistol, but assured us he had met with them in a pathway in the wood, and protested that he had not been able to meet with any one of his countrymen. This report had so little the air of truth, that we suspected there was some treachery carrying on, and therefore, to prevent any future communication amongst them, we immediately ordered all the Indians who were in our power on board the ship, and did not permit them to return any more on shore.

When our sick were well settled on the island, we employed all the hands that could be spared from attending them, in arming the cables with a good rounding several fathoms from the anchor, to secure them from being rubbed by the coral rocks which here abounded. And this being completed, our next attention was our leak, and in order to raise it out of water, we, on the first of September, began to get the guns aft to bring the ship by the stern; and now the carpenters, being able to come at it on the outside, ripped off the old sheathing that was left, and caulked all the seams on both sides the cut-water and leaded them over, and then new sheathed the bows to the surface of the water. By this means we conceived the defect was sufficiently secured; but upon our beginning to bring the guns into their places, we had the mortification to perceive that the water rushed into the ship in the old place with as much violence as ever. Hereupon we were necessitated to begin again; and that our second attempt might be more effectual we cleared the fore-storeroom, and sent a hundred and thirty barrels of powder on board the small Spanish bark we had seized here, by which means we raised the ship about three feet out of the water forwards, and the carpenters ripped off the sheathing lower down, and new caulked all the seams, and afterwards laid on new sheathing; and then, supposing the leak to be effectually stopped, we began to move the guns forwards; but the upper deck guns were scarcely in their places, when, to our amazement, it burst out again; and now, as we durst not cut away the lining within-board, lest a but-end or a plank might start, and we might go down immediately, we had no other resource left than chincing and caulking within-board; and indeed by this means the leak was stopped for some time; but when our guns were all in their places, and our stores were taken on board, the water again forced its way through a hole in the stem, where one of the bolts was driven in; and on this we desisted from all further efforts, being now well assured that the defect was in the stem itself, and that it was not to be remedied till we should have an opportunity of heaving down.

Towards the middle of September several of our siok were tolerably recovered by their residence on shore; and on the 12th of September all those who were so far relieved, since their arrival, as to be capable of doing duty were sent on board the ship. And then the commodore, who was himself ill of the scurvy, had a tent erected for him on shore, where he went with the view of staying a few days for the recovery of his health, being convinced, by the general experience of his people, that

no other method but living on the land was to be trusted
to for the removal of this dreadful malady. The place
where his tent was pitched on this occasion was near the
well, whence we got all our water, and was indeed a most
elegant spot.

As the crew on board were now reinforced by the
recovered hands returned from the island, we began to
send our casks on shore to be fitted up, which till now
could not be done, for the coopers were not well enough to
work. We likewise weighed our anchors that we might
examine our cables, which we suspected had by this
time received considerable damage. And as the new
moon was now approaching, when we apprehended
violent gales, the commodore, for our greater security,
ordered that part of the cables next to the anchors to be
armed with the chains of the fire-grapnels; and they
were besides cackled twenty fathoms from the anchors,
and seven fathoms from the service, with a good rounding
of a $4\frac{1}{2}$ inch hawser; and to all these precautions we
added that of lowering the main and foreyard close
down, that in case of blowing weather the wind might
have less power upon the ship to make her ride a strain.

Thus effectually prepared, as we conceived, we expected the new moon, which was the 18th of September,
and riding safe that and the three succeeding days (though
the weather proved very squally and uncertain), we
flattered ourselves (for I was then on board) that the
prudence of our measures had secured us from all
accidents; but on the 22nd the wind blew from the
eastward with such fury, that we soon despaired of riding
out the storm; and therefore we should have been
extremely glad that the commodore and the rest of our

people on shore, which were the greatest part of our
hands, had been on board with us, since our only hopes
of safety seemed to depend on our putting immediately
to sea; but all communication with the shore was now
effectually cut off, for there was no possibility that a boat
could live, so that we were necessitated to ride it out till
our cables parted.   Indeed it was not long before this
happened, for the small bower parted at five in the afternoon, and the ship swung off to the best bower; and as
the night came on the violence of the wind still increased;
but, notwithstanding its inexpressible fury, the tide ran
with so much rapidity as to prevail over it; for the tide
having set to the northward in the beginning of the
storm, turned suddenly to the southward about six in
the evening, and forced the ship before it in despite of
the storm which blew upon the beam.   And now the
sea broke most surprisingly all round us, and a large
tumbling swell threatened to poop us; the long-boat,
which was at this time moored a-stern, was on a sudden
canted so high, that it broke the transom of the commodore's gallery, whose cabin was on the quarter-deck,
and would doubtless have risen as high as the tafferel,
had it not been for this stroke which stove the boat all
to pieces; but the poor boatkeeper, though extremely
bruised, was saved almost by miracle.   About eight the
tide slackened, but the wind did not abate; so that at
eleven the best bower cable, by which alone we rode,
parted.   Our sheet anchor, which was the only one we
had left, was instantly cut from the bow; but before it
could reach the bottom we were driven from twenty-two
into thirty-five fathoms; and after we had veered away
one whole cable, and two thirds of another, we could not

find ground with sixty fathom of line. This was a plain
indication that the anchor lay near the edge of the bank,
and could not hold us long. In this pressing danger,
Mr. Saumarez, our first lieutenant, who now commanded
on board, ordered several guns to be fired, and lights to
be shown, as a signal to the commodore of our distress;
and in a short time after, it being then about one o'clock,
and the night excessively dark, a strong gust, attended
with rain and lightning, drove us off the bank and forced
us out to sea, leaving behind us on the island, Mr. Anson,
with many more of our officers, and great part of our
crew, amounting in the whole to a hundred and thirteen
persons. Thus were we all, both at sea and on shore,
reduced to the utmost despair by this catastrophe; those
on shore conceiving they had no means left them ever to
leave the island, and we on board utterly unprepared to
struggle with the fury of the seas and winds we were now
exposed to, and expecting each moment to be our last.

CHAPTER III

Transactions at Tinian after the departure of the
Centurion.

THE storm which drove the Centurion to sea blew
with too much turbulence to permit either the commodore
or any of the people on shore to hear the guns, which
she fired as signals of distress; and the frequent glare of
the lightning had prevented the explosions from being
observed. So that, when at daybreak, it was perceived
from the shore that the ship was missing, there was the
utmost consternation amongst them. For much the
greatest part of them immediately concluded that she
was lost, and intreated the commodore that the boat
might be sent round the island to look for the wreck;
and those who believed her safe, had scarcely any
expectation that she would ever be able to make the island
again. For the wind continued to blow strong at east,
and they knew how poorly she was manned and provided
for struggling with so tempestuous a gale. And if the
Centurion was lost, or should be incapable of returning,
there appeared in either case no possibility of their ever
getting off the island; for they were at least six hundred
leagues from Macao, which was their nearest port; and

they were masters of no other vessel than the small Spanish bark of about fifteen tons which they seized at their first arrival, and which would not even hold a fourth part of their number. And the chance of their being taken off the island by the casual arrival of any other ship was altogether desperate; as perhaps no European ship had ever anchored here before, and it were madness to expect that like incidents should send another here in a hundred ages to come. So that their desponding thoughts could only suggest to them the melancholy prospect of spending the remainder of their days on this island, and bidding adieu for ever to their country, their friends, their families, and all their domestic endearments.

Nor was this the worst they had to fear : for they had reason to expect that the governor of Guam, when he should be informed of their situation, might send a force sufficient to overpower them, and to remove them to that island; and then, the most favourable treatment they could hope for would be to be detained prisoners for life; since, from the known policy and cruelty of the Spaniards in their distant settlements, it was rather to be expected that the governor, if he once had them in his power, would make their want of commissions (all of them being on board the Centurion) a pretext for treating them as pirates, and for depriving them of their lives with infamy.

In the midst of these gloomy reflections, Mr. Anson had doubtless his share of disquietude; but he always kept up his usual composure and steadiness : and having soon projected a scheme for extricating himself and his men from their present anxious situation, he first communicated it to some of the most intelligent persons about him; and having satisfied himself that it was practicable, he then endeavoured to animate his people to a speedy and vigorous prosecution of it. With this view he represented to them how little foundation there was for their apprehensions of the Centurion's being lost: that he should have hoped they had been all of them better acquainted with sea affairs than to give way to the impression of so chimerical a fright; and that he doubted not, but if they would seriously consider what such a ship was capable of enduring, they would confess that there was not the least probability of her having perished: that he was not without hopes that she might return in a few days; but if she did not, the worst that could be supposed was, that she was driven so far to the leeward of the island that she could not regain it, and that she would consequently be obliged to bear away for Macao on the coast of China: that as it was necessary to be prepared against all events, he had, in this case, considered of a method of carrying them off the island, and joining their old ship the Centurion again at Macao: that this method was to hale the Spanish bark on shore, to saw her asunder, and to lengthen her twelve feet, which would enlarge her to near forty tons burthen, and would enable her to carry them all to China: that he had consulted the carpenters, and they had agreed that this proposal was very feasible, and that nothing was wanting to execute it but the united resolution and industry of the whole body: he added, that for his own part, he would share the fatigue and labour with them, and would expect no more from any man than what he, the commodore himself, was ready to submit to; and concluded with representing to them the importance of

saving time; and that, in order to be the better prepared
for all events, it was necessary to set to work immediately,
and to take it for granted that the Centurion would not
be able to put back (which was indeed the commodore's
secret opinion); since, if she did return, they should only
throw away a few days' application; but, if she did not,
their situation, and the season of the year, required their
utmost despatch.

These remonstrances, though not without effect, did
not immediately operate so powerfully as Mr. Anson
could have wished: he indeed raised their spirits by
showing them the possibility of their getting away, of
which they had before despaired; but then, from their
confidence of this resource, they grew less apprehensive
of their situation, gave a greater scope to their hopes, and
flattered themselves that the Centurion would return and
prevent the execution of the commodore's scheme, which
they could easily foresee would be a work of considerable
labour: by this means it was some days before they were
all of them heartily engaged in the project; but at last,
being in general convinced of the impossibility of the
ship's return, they set themselves zealously to the different
tasks allotted them, and were as industrious and as eager
as their commander could desire, punctually assembling
at daybreak at the rendezvous, whence they were distributed to their different employments, which they
followed with unusual vigour till night came on.

If we examine how they were prepared for going
through with this undertaking, on which their safety
depended, we shall find that, independent of other
matters which were of as much importance, the lengthen-
ing of the bark alone was attended with great difficulty.

Indeed, in a proper place, where all the necessary materials and tools were to be had, the embarrassment would have been much less; but some of these tools were to be made, and many of the materials were wanting, and it required no small degree of invention to supply all these deficiencies. And when the hull of the bark should be completed this was but one article, and there were many others of equal weight which were to be well considered: these were the rigging it, the victualling it, and, lastly, the navigating it for the space of six or seven hundred leagues, through unknown seas, where no one of the company had ever passed before. In some of these particulars such obstacles occurred that, without the intervention of very extraordinary and unexpected accidents, the possibility of the whole enterprise would have fallen to the ground, and their utmost industry and efforts must have been fruitless. Of all these circumstances I shall make a short recital.

It fortunately happened that the carpenters, both of the Gloucester and of the Tryal, with their chests of tools, were on shore when the ship drove out to sea; the smith too was on shore, and had with him his forge and some tools, but unhappily his bellows had not been brought from on board, so that he was incapable of working, and without his assistance they could not hope to proceed with their design. Their first attention therefore was to make him a pair of bellows, but in this they were for some time puzzled by their want of leather; however, as they had hides in sufficient plenty, and they had found a hogshead of lime, which the Indians or Spaniards had prepared for their own use, they tanned some hides with this lime; and though we may suppose the workmanship to be but indifferent, yet the leather they thus made served tolerably well, and the bellows (to which a gun-barrel served for a pipe) had no other inconvenience than that of being somewhat strong scented from the imperfection of the tanner's work.

Whilst the smith was preparing the necessary iron-work, others were employed in cutting down trees and sawing them into planks; and this being the most laborious task, the commodore wrought at it himself for the encouragement of his people. As there were neither blocks nor cordage sufficient for tackles to hale the bark on shore, it was proposed to get her up on rollers, and for these the body of the cocoa-nut tree was extremely useful, for its smoothness and circular turn prevented much labour, and fitted it for the purpose with very little workmanship: a number of these trees were therefore felled and the ends of them properly opened for the reception of handspikes, and in the meantime a dry dock was dug for the bark, and ways laid from thence quite into the sea, to facilitate the bringing her up. And besides those who were thus occupied in preparing measures for the future enlargement of the bark, a party was constantly ordered for the killing and preparing of provisions for the rest: and though in these various employments, some of which demanded considerable dexterity, it might have been expected there would have been great confusion and delay, yet good order being once established, and all hands engaged, their preparations advanced apace. Indeed the common men, I presume, were not the less tractable for their want of spirituous liquors; for, there being neither wine nor brandy on shore, the juice of the cocoa-nut was their constant drink, and this, though extremely pleasant, was not at all intoxicating, but kept them very cool and orderly.

And now the officers began to consider of all the articles necessary for the fitting out the bark; when it was found, that the tents on shore, and the spare cordage accidentally left there by the Centurion, together with the sails and rigging already belonging to the bark, would serve to rig her indifferently well, when she was lengthened: and as they had tallow in plenty, they proposed to pay her bottom with a mixture of tallow and lime, which it was known was well adapted to that purpose: so that with respect to her equipment, she would not have been very defective. There was, however, one exception, which would have proved extremely inconvenient, and that was her size: for as they could not make her quite forty tons burthen, she would have been incapable of containing half the crew below the deck, and she would have been so top-heavy that if they were all at the same time ordered upon deck there would be no small hazard of her oversetting; but this was a difficulty not to be removed, as they could not augment her beyond the size already proposed. After the manner of rigging and fitting up the bark was considered and regulated, the next essential point to be thought on was, how to procure a sufficient stock of provisions for their voyage; and here they were greatly at a loss what course to take; for they had neither grain nor bread of any kind on shore, their bread-fruit, which would not keep at sea, having all along supplied its place: and though they had live cattle enough, yet they had no salt to cure beef for a sea-store, nor would meat take salt in that climate. Indeed, they had preserved a small quantity of jerked beef, which they found upon the place at their landing; but this was greatly disproportioned to the run of near six hundred leagues, which they were to engage in, and to the number of hands they should have on board. It was at last, however, resolved to take on board as many cocoa-nuts as they possibly could; to make the most of their jerked beef, by a very sparing distribution of it; and to endeavour to supply their want of bread by rice; to furnish themselves with which, it was proposed, when the bark was fitted up, to make an expedition to the island of Rota, where they were told that the Spaniards had large plantations of rice under the care of the Indian inhabitants: but as this last measure was to be executed by force, it became necessary to examine what ammunition had been left on shore, and to preserve it carefully; and on this inquiry, they had the mortification to find that the utmost that could be collected by the strictest search did not amount to more than ninety charges of powder for their firelocks, which was considerably short of one apiece for each of the company, and was indeed a very slender stock of ammunition, for such as were to eat no grain or bread for a month, but what they were to procure by force of arms.

But the most alarming circumstance, and what, without the providential interposition of very improbable events, had rendered all their schemes abortive, remains yet to be related. The general idea of the fabric and equipment of the vessel was settled in a few days; and when this was done it was not difficult to make some estimation of the time necessary to complete her. After this, it was natural to expect that the officers would consider

on the course they were to steer, and the land they were
to make. These reflections led them to the dishearten-
ing discovery, that there was neither compass nor
quadrant on the island. Indeed the commodore had
brought a pocket-compass on shore for his own use; but
Lieutenant Brett had borrowed it to determine the
position of the neighbouring islands, and he had been
driven to sea in the Centurion, without returning it: and
as to a quadrant, that could not be expected to be found
on shore, for as it was of no use at land, there could be
no reason for bringing it from on board the ship. It
was eight days, from the departure of the Centurion,
before they were in any degree relieved from this terrible
perplexity: at last, in rummaging a chest belonging to
the Spanish bark, they found a small compass, which,
though little better than the toys usually made for the
amusement of schoolboys, was to them an invaluable
treasure. And a few days after, by a similar piece of
good fortune, they found a quadrant on the seashore,
which had been thrown overboard amongst other lumber
belonging to the dead: the quadrant was eagerly seized,
but on examination, it unluckily wanted vanes, and therefore in its present state was altogether useless; however,
fortune still continuing in a favourable mood, it was not
long before a person out of curiosity pulling out the
drawer of an old table, which had been driven on shore,
found therein some vanes, which fitted the quadrant
very well; and it being thus completed, it was examined
by the known latitude of the place, and was found to
answer to a sufficient degree of exactness.

And now, all these obstacles being in some degree
removed (which were always as much as possible con-

cealed from the vulgar, that they might not grow remiss
with the apprehension of labouring to no purpose), the
work proceeded very successfully and vigorously: the
necessary ironwork was in great forwardness; and the
timbers and planks (which, though not the most exquisite
performances of the sawyer's art, were yet sufficient for
the purpose) were all prepared; so that, on the 6th of
October, being the fourteenth day from the departure of
the ship, they haled the bark on shore, and on the two
succeeding days she was sawn asunder (though with
great care not to cut her planks), and her two parts were
separated the proper distance from each other, and, the
materials being all ready beforehand, they, the next day,
being the 9th of October, went on with great despatch
in their proposed enlargement of her; and by this time
they had all their future operations so fairly in view, and
were so much masters of them, that they were able to
determine when the whole would be finished, and had
accordingly fixed the 5th of November for the day of
their putting to sea. But their projects and labours were
now drawing to a speedier and happier conclusion; for
on the 11th of October, in the afternoon, one of the
Gloucester's men, being upon a hill in the middle of the
island, perceived the Centurion at a distance, and running
down with his utmost speed towards the landing-place,
he, in the way, saw some of his comrades, to whom he
hallooed out with great ecstasy, "The ship, the ship!"
This being heard by Mr. Gordon, a lieutenant of
marines, who was convinced by the fellow's transport
that his report was true, Mr. Gordon ran towards the
place where the commodore and his people were at work,
and being fresh and in breath, easily outstripped the

Gloucester's man, and got before him to the commodore, who, on hearing this happy and unexpected news, threw down his axe with which he was then at work, and by his joy broke through, for the first time, the equable and unvaried character which he had hitherto preserved; the others, who were with him, instantly ran down to the seaside in a kind of frenzy, eager to feast themselves with a sight they had so ardently wished for, and of which they had now for a considerable time despaired. By five in the evening, the Centurion was visible in the offing to them all; and, a boat being sent off with eighteen men to reinforce her, and with fresh meat and fruits for the refreshment of her crew, she, the next afternoon, happily came to an anchor in the road, where the commodore immediately came on board her, and was received by us with the sincerest and heartiest acclamations: for, from the following short recital of the fears, the dangers' and fatigues we in the ship underwent during our nineteen days' absence from Tinian, it may be easily conceived that a harbour, refreshments, repose, and the joining of our commander and shipmates, were not less pleasing to us, than our return was to them.

CHAPTER IV

Proceedings on board the Centurion, when driven out
to sea.

THE Centurion being now once more safely arrived at
Tinian, to the mutual respite of the labours of our
divided crew, it is high time that the reader, after the
relation already given of the projects and employment of
those left on shore, should be apprised of the fatigues
and distresses, to which we, who were driven off to sea,
were exposed during the long interval of nineteen days
that we were absent from the island.

It has been already mentioned, that it was the 22nd
of September, about one o'clock, in an extremely dark
night, when by the united violence of a prodigious
storm, and an exceeding rapid tide, we were driven from
our anchors and forced to sea. Our condition then was
truly deplorable; we were in a leaky ship, with three
cables in our hawses, to one of which hung our only
remaining anchor; we had not a gun on board lashed,
nor a port barred in; our shrouds were loose, and our
topmasts unrigged, and we had struck our fore and main-
yards close down before the storm came on, so that there
were no sails we could set, except our mizen.

45

In this dreadful extremity we could muster no more strength on board, to navigate the ship, than a hundred and eight hands, several negroes and Indians included: this was scarcely the fourth part of our complement; and of these the greater number were either boys, or such as, being lately recovered from the scurvy, had not yet arrived at half their former vigour. No sooner were we at sea, but by the violence of the storm, and the working of the ship, we made a great quantity of water through our hawse-holes, ports and scuppers, which, added to the constant effect of our leak, rendered our pumps alone a sufficient employment for us all: but though this leakage, by being a short time neglected, would inevitably end in our destruction, yet we had other dangers then impending, which occasioned this to be regarded as a secondary consideration only. For we all imagined that we were driving directly on the neighbouring island of Aguiguan, which was about two leagues distant; and as we had lowered our main and foreyards close down, we had no sails we could set but the mizen, which was altogether insufficient to carry us clear of this instant peril: we therefore immediately applied ourselves to work, endeavouring, by the utmost of our efforts, to heave up the main and foreyards, in hopes that, if we could but be enabled to make use of our lower canvas, we might possibly weather the island, and thereby save ourselves from this impending shipwreck. But after full three hours' ineffectual labour, the jeers broke, and the men being quite jaded, we were obliged, by mere debility, to desist, and quietly to expect our fate, which we then conceived to be unavoidable: for we imagined ourselves by this time to be driven just

upon the shore, and the night was so extremely dark
that we expected to discover the island no otherwise
than by striking upon it; so that the belief of our
destruction, and the uncertainty of the point of time
when it would take place, occasioned us to pass several
hours under the most serious apprehensions that each
succeeding moment would send us to the bottom. Nor
did these continued terrors, of instantly striking and
sinking, end but with the daybreak; when we with great
transport perceived that the island we had thus dreaded
was at a considerable distance, and that a strong northern
current had been the cause of our preservation.

The turbulent weather, which forced us from Tinian,
did not begin to abate till three days after; and then we
swayed up the foreyard, and began to heave up the
mainyard, but the jeers broke and killed one of our
men, and prevented us at that time from proceeding.
The next day, being the 26th of September, was a day
of most severe fatigue to us all; for it must be remembered,
that in these exigences no rank or office exempted any
person from the manual application and bodily labour of
a common sailor. The business of this day was no less
than an attempt to heave up the sheet-anchor, which we
had hitherto dragged at our bows with two cables an
end. This was a work of great importance to our future
preservation. For, not to mention the impediment to
our navigation, and the hazard it would be to our ship,
if we attempted to make sail with the anchor in its
present situation, we had this most interesting consideration to animate us, that it was the only anchor we had
left; and, without securing it, we should be under the
utmost difficulties and hazards whenever we made the

land again; and therefore being all of us fully apprised of the consequence of this enterprise, we laboured at it with the severest application for full twelve hours, when we had indeed made a considerable progress, having brought the anchor in sight; but it then growing dark, and we being excessively fatigued, we were obliged to desist, and to leave our work unfinished till the next morning, when, by the benefit of a night's rest, we completed and hung the anchor at our bow.

It was the 27th of September, in the morning, that is five days after our departure, when we thus secured our anchor; and the same day we got up our mainyard. And having now conquered, in some degree, the distress and disorder which we were necessarily involved in at our first driving out to sea, and being enabled to make use of our canvas, we set our courses, and for the first time stood to the eastward, in hopes of regaining the island of Tinian, and joining our commodore in a few days. For we were then, by our accounts, only forty-seven leagues to the south-west of Tinian; so that on the first day of October, having then run the distance necessary for making the island according to our reckoning, we were in full expectation of seeing it; but we were unhappily disappointed, and were thereby convinced that a current had driven us to the westward. And as we could not judge how much we might hereby have deviated, and, consequently, how long we might still expect to be at sea, we had great apprehensions that our stock of water might prove deficient; for we were doubtful about the quantity we had on board, and found many of our casks so decayed as to be half-leaked out. However, we were delivered from our uncertainty the next day by having a sight of the island of Guam, by which we discovered that the currents had driven us forty-four leagues to the westward of our accounts. This sight of land having satisfied us of our situation, we kept plying to the eastward, though with excessive labour, for the wind continuing fixed in the eastern board, we were obliged to tack often, and our crew were so weak, that, without the assistance of every man on board, it was not in our power to put the ship about. This severe employment lasted till the 11th of October, being the nineteenth day from our departure; when arriving in the offing of Tinian, we were reinforced from the shore, as hath been already mentioned; and on the evening of the same day, we, to our inexpressible joy, came to an anchor in the road, thereby procuring to our shipmates on shore, as well as to ourselves, a cessation from the fatigues and apprehensions which this disastrous incident had given rise to.

CHAPTER V

Employment at Tinian, till the final departure of the
  Centurion from thence; with a description of the
  Ladrones.

WHEN the commodore came on board the Centurion,
on her return to Tinian, as already mentioned, he
resolved to stay no longer at the island than was
absolutely necessary to complete our stock of water, a
work which we immediately set ourselves about. But
the loss of our long-boat, which was staved against our
poop, when we were driven out to sea, put us to great
inconveniences in getting our water on board; for we
were obliged to raft off all our casks, and the tide ran so
strong, that, besides the frequent delays and difficulties
it occasioned, we more than once lost the whole raft.
Nor was this our only misfortune; for, on the 14th of
October, being but the third day after our arrival, a
sudden gust of wind brought home our anchor, forced
us off the bank, and drove the ship out to sea a second
time. The commodore, it is true, and the principal
officers, were now on board; but we had near seventy
men on shore, who had been employed in filling our
water, and procuring provisions. These had with them

our two cutters; but as they were too many for the
cutters to bring off at once, we sent the eighteen-oared
barge to assist them; and at the same time made a
signal for all that could to embark. The two cutters
soon came off to us full of men; but forty of the
company, who were employed in killing cattle in the
wood, and in bringing them down to the landing-place,
were left behind; and though the eighteen-oared barge
was left for their conveyance, yet, as the ship soon drove
to a considerable distance, it was not in their power to
join us. However, as the weather was favourable, and
our crew was now stronger than when we were first
driven out, we, in about five days' time, returned again
to an anchor at Tinian, and relieved those we had left
behind us from their second fears of being deserted by
their ship.

On our arrival, we found that the Spanish bark, the
old object of their hopes, had undergone a new meta-
morphosis. For those we had left on shore began to
despair of our return; and conceiving that the lengthen-
ing the bark, as formerly proposed, was both a toilsome
and unnecessary measure, considering the small number
they consisted of, they had resolved to join her again,
and to restore her to her first state; and in this scheme
they had made some progress; for they had brought the
two parts together, and would have soon completed her,
had not our coming back put a period to their labours
and disquietudes.

These people we had left behind informed us that,
just before we were seen in the offing, two proas had
stood in very near the shore, and had continued there
for some time; but on the appearance of our ship, they

crowded away, and were presently out of sight. And,
on this occasion I must mention an incident, which,
though it happened during the first absence of the ship,
was then omitted, to avoid interrupting the course of the
narration.

It hath already been observed that a part of the
detachment sent to this island, under the command of
the Spanish sergeant, lay concealed in the woods; and
we were the less solicitous to find them out, as our
prisoners all assured us that it was impossible for them
to get off, and, consequently, that it was impossible for
them to send any intelligence about us to Guam. But
when the Centurion drove out to sea, and left the
commodore on shore, he one day, attended by some of
his officers, endeavoured to make the tour of the island.
In this expedition, being on a rising ground, they perceived in the valley beneath them the appearance of a
small thicket, which, by observing more nicely, they
found had a progressive motion. This at first surprised
them; but they soon discovered that it was no more
than several large cocoa-bushes, which were dragged
along the ground by persons concealed beneath them.
They immediately concluded that these were some of
the sergeant's party (which was indeed true); and therefore the commodore and his people made after them,
in hopes of finding out their retreat. The Indians soon
perceived they were discovered, and hurried away with
precipitation; but Mr. Anson was so near them, that he
did not lose sight of them till they arrived at their cell,
which he and his officers entering found to be abandoned,
there being a passage from it down a precipice contrived
for the convenience of flight. They found here an old

firelock or two, but no other arms. However, there was
a great quantity of provisions, particularly salted spareribs
of pork, which were excellent; and from what our
people saw here, they concluded that the extraordinary
appetite which they had found at this island was not
confined to themselves alone; for, it being about noon,
the Indians had laid out a very plentiful repast, considering their numbers, and had their bread-fruit and
cocoa-nuts prepared ready for eating, and in a manner
which plainly evinced that, with them too, a good meal
was neither an uncommon nor an unheeded article.
The commodore having in vain endeavoured to discover
the path by which the Indians had escaped, he and his
officers contented themselves with sitting down to the
dinner which was thus luckily fitted to their present
appetites; after which they returned back to their old
habitation, displeased at missing the Indians, as they
hoped to have engaged them in our service, if they could
have had any conference with them. But notwithstanding what our prisoners had asserted, we were afterwards
assured that these Indians were carried off to Guam
long before we left the place. But to return to our
history.

On our coming to an anchor again, after our second
driving off to sea, we laboured indefatigably in getting
in our water; and having, by the 20th of October,
completed it to fifty tons, which we supposed would be
sufficient for our passage to Macao, we, on the next day,
sent one of each mess on shore to gather as large a
quantity of oranges, lemons, cocoa-nuts, and other fruits
of the island, as they possibly could, for the use of
themselves and messmates, when at sea. And these

purveyors returning on board us on the evening of the
same day, we then set fire to the bark and proa, hoisted
in our boats, and got under sail, steering away for the
south end of the island of Formosa, and taking our
leaves, for the third and last time, of the island of
Tinian: an island which, whether we consider the
excellence of its productions, the beauty of its appearance, the elegance of its woods and lawns, the healthiness of its air, or the adventures it gave rise to, may in
all these views be truly styled romantic.

CHAPTER VI

From Tinian to Macao.

I HAVE already mentioned, that, on the 21st of October, in the evening, we took our leave of the island of Tinian, steering the proper course for Macao in China. The eastern monsoon was now, we reckoned, fairly settled; and we had a constant gale blowing right upon our stern: so that we generally ran from forty to fifty leagues a day. But we had a large hollow sea pursuing us, which occasioned the ship to labour much; whence we received great damage in our rigging, which was grown very rotten, and our leak was augmented: but happily for us, our people were now in full health; so that there were no complaints of fatigue, but all went through their attendance on the pumps, and every other duty of the ship, with ease and cheerfulness.

Having now no other but our sheet-anchor left, except our prize-anchors, which were stowed in the hold, and were too light to be depended on, we were under great concern how we should manage on the coast of China, where we were all entire strangers, and where we should doubtless be frequently under the necessity of coming to an anchor. Our sheet-anchor being obviously much too heavy for a coasting-anchor, it was at length resolved to fix two of our largest prize-anchors into one stock, and to place between their shanks two guns, four pounders, which was accordingly executed, and it was to serve as a best bower: and a third prize-anchor being in like manner joined with our stream-anchor, with guns between them, we thereby made a small bower; so that, besides our sheet-anchor, we had again two others at our bows, one of which weighed 3900, and the other 2900 pounds.

The 3rd of November, about three in the afternoon, we saw an island, which at first we imagined to be the island of Botel Tobago Ximo: but on our nearer approach we found it to be much smaller than that is usually represented; and about an hour after we saw another island, five or six miles farther to the westward. As no chart, nor any journal we had seen, took notice of any other island to the eastward of Formosa than Botel Tobago Ximo, and as we had no observation of our latitude at noon, we were in some perplexity, being apprehensive that an extraordinary current had driven us into the neighbourhood of the Bashee islands; and therefore, when night came on, we brought to, and continued in this posture till the next morning, which proving dark and cloudy, for some time prolonged our uncertainty; but it cleared up about nine o'clock, when we again discerned the two islands above-mentioned; we then pressed forward to the westward, and by eleven got sight of the southern part of the island of Formosa. This satisfied us that the second island we saw was Botel Tobago Ximo, and the first a small island or rock, lying five or six miles due east from it, which, not being mentioned by any of our books or charts, was the occasion of our fears.

When we got sight of the island of Formosa, we steered W. by S. in order to double its extremity, and kept a good look-out for the rocks of Vele Rete, which we did not see till two in the afternoon. They then bore from us W.N.W., three miles distant, the south end of Formosa at the same time bearing N. by W. ½ W., about five leagues distant. To give these rocks a good berth, we immediately hauled up S. by W., and so left them between us and the land. Indeed we had reason to be careful of them; for though they appeared as high out of the water as a ship's hull, yet they are environed with breakers on all sides, and there is a shoal stretching from them at least a mile and a half to the southward, whence they may be truly called dangerous. The course from Botel Tobago Ximo to these rocks is S.W. by W., and the distance about twelve or thirteen leagues: and the south end of Formosa, off which they lie, is in the latitude of 21° 50′ north, and in 23° 50′ west longitude from Tinian, according to our most approved reckonings, though by some of our accounts above a degree more.

While we were passing by these rocks of Vele Rete, there was an outcry of fire on the forecastle; this occasioned a general alarm, and the whole crew instantly flocked together in the utmost confusion, so that the officers found it difficult for some time to appease the uproar: but having at last reduced the people to order, it was perceived that the fire proceeded from the furnace; and pulling down the brick-work, it was extinguished with great facility, for it had taken its rise from the bricks, which, being over-heated, had begun to communicate the fire to the adjacent wood-work. In the evening we were surprised with a view of what we at first sight conceived to have been breakers, but, on a stricter examination, we found them to be only a great number of fires on the island of Formosa. These, we imagined, were intended by the inhabitants of that island as signals for us to touch there, but that suited not our views, we being impatient to reach the port of Macao as soon as possible. From Formosa we steered W.N.W., and sometimes still more northerly, proposing to fall in with the coast of China, to the eastward of Pedro Blanco; for the rock so called is usually esteemed an excellent direction for ships bound to Macao. We continued this course till the following night, and then frequently brought to, to try if we were in soundings: but it was the 5th of November, at nine in the morning, before we struck ground, and then we had forty-two fathoms, and a bottom of grey sand mixed with shells. When we had got about twenty miles farther W.N.W., we had thirty-five fathoms, and the same bottom, from whence our soundings gradually decreased from thirty-five to twenty-five fathoms; but soon after, to our great surprise, they jumped back again to thirty fathoms: this was an alteration we could not very well account for, since all the charts laid down regular soundings everywhere to the northward of Pedro Blanco ; and for this reason we kept a very careful lookout, and altered our course to N.N.W., and having ran thirty-five miles in this direction, our soundings again gradually diminished to twenty-two fathoms, and we at last, about midnight, got sight of the mainland of China, bearing N. by W., four leagues distant: we then brought the ship to, with her head to the sea, proposing to wait for the morning; and before sunrise we were surprised to find ourselves in the midst of an incredible number of fishing-boats, which seemed to cover the surface of the sea as far as the eye could reach. I may well style their number incredible, since I cannot believe, upon the lowest estimate, that there were so few as six thousand, most of them manned with five hands, and none of those we saw with less than three. Nor was this swarm of fishing-vessels peculiar to this spot; for, as we ran on to the westward, we found them as abundant on every part of the coast. We at first doubted not but we should procure a pilot from them to carry us to Macao; but though many of them came close to the ship, and we endeavoured to tempt them by showing them a number of dollars, a most alluring bait for Chinese of all ranks and professions, yet we could not entice them on board us, nor procure any directions from them; though, I presume, the only difficulty was their not comprehending what we wanted them to do, for we could have no communication with them but by signs: indeed we often pronounced the word Macao; but this we had reason to suppose they understood in a different sense; for in return they sometimes held up fish to us, and we afterwards learnt that the Chinese name for fish is of a somewhat similar sound. But what surprised us most was the inattention and want of curiosity, which we observed in this herd of fishermen: a ship like ours had doubtless never been in those seas before; perhaps there might not be one amongst all the Chinese employed in this fishery who had ever seen any European vessel; so that we might reasonably have expected to have been considered by them as a very uncommon and extraordinary object; but though many of their vessels came close to the ship, yet they did not appear to be at all interested about us, nor did they deviate in the least from their course to regard us; which insensibility, especially in maritime persons, about a matter in their own profession, is scarcely to be credited, did not the general behaviour of the Chinese, in other instances, furnish us with continual proofs of a similar turn of mind: it may perhaps be doubted whether this cast of temper be the effect of nature or education; but, in either case, it is an incontestible symptom of a mean and contemptible disposition, and is alone a sufficient confutation of the extravagant panegyrics, which many hypothetical writers have bestowed on the ingenuity and capacity of this nation. But to return.

Not being able to procure any information from the Chinese fishermen about our proper course to Macao, it was necessary for us to rely entirely on our own judgment; and concluding from our latitude, which was 22° 42′ North, and from our soundings, which were only seventeen or eighteen fathoms, that we were yet to the eastward of Pedro Blanco, we stood to the westward: and for the assistance of future navigators, who may hereafter doubt about the parts of the coast they are upon, I must observe, that besides the latitude of Pedro Blanco, which is 22° 18′, and the depth of water, which to the westward of that rock is almost everywhere twenty fathoms, there is another circumstance which will give great assistance in judging of the position of the ship: this is the kind of ground; for, till we came within thirty miles of Pedro Blanco, we had constantly a sandy bottom; but there the bottom changed to soft and muddy, and continued so quite to the island of Macao; only while we were in sight of Pedro Blanco, and very near it, we had for a short space a bottom of greenish mud, intermixed with sand.

It was on the 5th of November, at midnight, when we first made the coast of China; and the next day, about two o'clock, as we were standing to the westward within two leagues of the coast, and still surrounded by fishing-vessels in as great numbers as at first, we perceived that a boat ahead of us waved a red flag, and blew a horn: this we considered as a signal made to us, either to warn us of some shoal, or to inform us that they would supply us with a pilot, and in this belief we immediately sent our cutter to the boat to know their intentions; but we were soon made sensible of our mistake, and found that this boat was the commodore of the whole fishery, and that the signal she had made was to order them all to leave off fishing, and to return in shore, which we saw them instantly obey. On this disappointment we kept on our course, and soon after passed by two very small rocks, which lay four or five miles distant from the shore; but night came on before we got sight of Pedro Blanco, and we therefore brought to till the morning, when we had the satisfaction to discover it. It is a rock of a small circumference, but of a moderate height, and, both in shape and colour, resembles a sugar-loaf, and is about seven or eight miles from the shore. We passed within a mile and a half of it, and left it between us and the land, still keeping on to the westward; and the next day, being the 7th, we were abreast of a chain of islands, which stretched from east to west. These, as we afterwards found, were called the islands of Lema; they are rocky and barren, and are in all, small and great, fifteen or sixteen; and there are, besides, a great number of other islands between them and the mainland of China.   These islands we left on the starboard side, passing within four miles of them, where we had twenty-four fathom water.   We were still surrounded by fishing-boats; and we once more sent the cutter on board one of them to endeavour to procure a pilot, but could not prevail; however one of the Chinese directed us by signs to sail round the westernmost of the islands or rocks of Lema, and then to hale up.   We followed this direction, and in the evening came to an anchor in eighteen fathoms.

After having continued at anchor all night, we on the 9th, at four in the morning, sent our cutter to sound the channel, where we proposed to pass; but before the return of the cutter, a Chinese pilot put on board us, and told us, in broken Portuguese, he would carry us to Macao for thirty dollars.   These were immediately paid him, and we then weighed and made sail; and soon after several other pilots came on board us, who, to recommend themselves, produced certificates from the captains of several ships they had piloted in, but we continued the ship under the management of the Chinese who came first on board.   By this time we learned that we were not far distant from Macao, and that there were in the river of Canton, at the mouth of which Macao lies, eleven European ships, of which four were English. Our pilot carried us between the islands of Bamboo and Cabouce, but the winds hanging in the northern board, and the tides often setting strongly against us, we were obliged to come frequently to an anchor, so that we did not get through between the two islands till the 12th of November, at two in the morning. In passing through, our depth of water was from twelve to fourteen fathoms: and as we still steered on N. by W. $\frac{1}{2}$ W., between a number of other islands, our soundings underwent little or no variation till towards the evening, when they increased to seventeen fathoms; in which depth (the wind dying away) we anchored not far from the island of Lantoon, which is the largest of all this range of islands. At seven in the morning we weighed again, and steering W.S.W. and S.W. by W., we at ten o'clock happily anchored in Macao road, in five fathom water, the city of Macao bearing W. by N., three leagues distant; the peak of Lantoon E. by N., and the grand Ladrone S. by E., each of them about five leagues distant. Thus, after a fatiguing cruise of above two years' continuance, we once more arrived in an amicable port in a civilised country; where the conveniences of life were in great plenty; where the naval stores, which we now extremely wanted, could be in some degree procured; where we expected the inexpressible satisfaction of receiving letters from our relations and friends; and where our country-men, who were lately arrived from England, would be capable of answering the numerous inquiries we were prepared to make, both about public and private occur-rences, and to relate to us many particulars, which, whether of importance or not, would be listened to by us with the utmost attention, after the long suspension of our correspondence with our country, to which the nature of our undertaking had hitherto subjected us.

CHAPTER VII

Proceedings at Macao.

THE city of Macao, in the road of which we came to an anchor on the 12th of November, is a Portuguese settlement, situated in an island at the mouth of the river of Canton. It was formerly a very rich and populous city, and capable of defending itself against the power of the adjacent Chinese governors; but at present it is much fallen from its ancient splendour; for though it is inhabited by Portuguese, and hath a governor nominated by the king of Portugal, yet it subsists merely by the sufferance of the Chinese, who can starve the place, and dispossess the Portuguese, whenever they please. This obliges the governor of Macao to behave with great circumspection, and carefully to avoid every circumstance that may give offence to the Chinese. The river of Canton, at the mouth of which this city lies, is the only Chinese port frequented by European ships; and this river is indeed a more commodious harbour, on many accounts, than Macao. But the peculiar customs of the Chinese, only adapted to the entertainment of trading ships, and the apprehensions of the commodore, lest he should embroil the East India Company with the regency of Canton, if he should insist on being treated upon a different footing than the merchantmen, made him resolve to go first to Macao, before he ventured into the port of Canton. Indeed, had not this reason prevailed with him, he himself had nothing to fear; for it is certain that he might have entered the port of Canton, and might have continued there as long as he pleased, and afterwards have left it again, although the whole power of the Chinese empire had been brought together to oppose him.

The commodore, not to depart from his usual prudence, no sooner came to an anchor in Macao road, than he despatched an officer with his compliments to the Portuguese governor of Macao, requesting his excellency, by the same officer, to advise him in what manner it would be proper to act to avoid offending the Chinese; which, as there were then four of our ships in their power at Canton, was a matter worthy of attention. The difficulty which the commodore principally apprehended, related to the duty usually paid by all ships in the river of Canton, according to their tonnage. For as men-of-war are exempted in every foreign harbour from all manner of port charges, the commodore thought it would be derogatory to the honour of his country, to submit to this duty in China: and therefore he desired the advice of the governor of Macao, who, being a European, could not be ignorant of the privileges claimed by a British man-of-war, and consequently might be expected to give us the best lights for avoiding this perplexity. Our boat returned in the evening with two officers, sent by the governor, who informed the commodore that it was the governor's opinion, that if the

Centurion ventured into the river of Canton, the duty would certainly be demanded; and, therefore, if the commodore approved of it, he would send him a pilot, who should conduct us into another safe harbour called the Typa, which was every way commodious for careening the ship (an operation we were resolved to begin upon as soon as possible), and where the above-mentioned duty would in all probability be never asked for.

This proposal the commodore agreed to, and in the morning we weighed anchor, and under the direction of the Portuguese pilot, steered for the intended harbour. As we entered two islands, which form the eastern passage to it, we found our soundings decreased to three fathoms and a half. But the pilot assuring us that this was the least depth we should meet with, we continued our course, till at length the ship stuck fast in the mud, with only eighteen foot water abaft; and the tide of ebb making, the water sewed to sixteen feet, but the ship remained perfectly upright; we then sounded all round us, and finding the water deepened to the northward, we carried out our small bower with two hawsers an end, and at the return of the tide of flood, hove the ship afloat; and a small breeze springing up at the same instant, we set the fore-topsail, and slipping the hawser, ran into the harbour, where we moored in about five fathom water. This harbour of the Typa is formed by a number of islands, and is about six miles distant from Macao. Here we saluted the castle of Macao with eleven guns, which were returned by an equal number.

The next day the commodore paid a visit in person to the governor, and was saluted at his landing by eleven guns; which were returned by the Centurion. Mr.

Anson's business in this visit was to solicit the governor to grant us a supply of provisions, and to furnish us with such stores as were necessary to refit the ship. The governor seemed really inclined to do us all the service he could, and assured the commodore, in a friendly manner, that he would privately give us all the assistance in his power; but he, at the same time, frankly owned that he dared not openly furnish us with anything we demanded, unless we first procured an order for it from the viceroy of Canton; for that he neither received provisions for his garrison, nor any other necessaries, but by permission from the Chinese government; and, as they took care only to furnish him from day to day, he was indeed no other than their vassal, whom they could at all times compel to submit to their own terms, only by laying an embargo on his provisions.

On this declaration of the governor, Mr. Anson resolved himself to go to Canton to procure a license from the viceroy; and he accordingly hired a Chinese boat for himself and his attendants; but just as he was ready to embark, the hoppo, or Chinese custom-house officer at Macao, refused to grant a permit to the boat, and ordered the watermen not to proceed, at their peril. The commodore at first endeavoured to prevail with the hoppo to withdraw his injunction, and to grant a permit; and the governor of Macao employed his interest with the hoppo to the same purpose. Mr. Anson, finding the officer inflexible, told him the next day, that if he longer refused to grant the permit, he would man and arm his own boats to carry him thither; asking the hoppo, at the same time, who he imagined would dare to oppose him. This threat immediately brought about what his

intreaties had laboured for in vain. The permit was
granted, and Mr. Anson went to Canton. On his arrival
there, he consulted with the super-cargoes and officers of
the English ships, how to procure an order from the
viceroy for the necessaries he wanted. But in this he
had reason to suppose that the advice they gave him,
though doubtless well intended, was yet not the most
prudent. For as it is the custom with these gentlemen
never to apply to the supreme magistrate himself, whatever difficulties they labour under, but to transact all
matters relating to the government by the mediation
of the principal Chinese merchants, Mr. Anson was
advised to follow the same method upon this occasion,
the English promising (in which they were doubtless
sincere) to exert all their interest to engage the merchants
in his favour. And when the Chinese merchants were
applied to, they readily undertook the management of it,
and promised to answer for its success; but after near
a month's delay, and reiterated excuses, during which
interval they pretended to be often upon the point of
completing the business, they at last (being pressed, and
measures being taken for delivering a letter to the viceroy)
threw off the mask, and declared they neither had applied
to the viceroy, nor could they; for he was too great a
man, they said, for them to approach on any occasion.
And, not contented with having themselves thus grossly
deceived the commodore, they now used all their persuasion with the English at Canton, to prevent them
from intermeddling with anything that regarded him,
representing to them that it would in all probability
embroil them with the government, and occasion them
a great deal of unnecessary trouble; which groundless

insinuations had indeed but too much weight with those they were applied to.

It may be difficult to assign a reason for this perfidious conduct of the Chinese merchants: interest indeed is known to exert a boundless influence over the inbabitants of that empire; but how their interest could be affected in the present case is not easy to discover; unless they apprehended that the presence of a ship of force might damp their Manila trade, and therefore acted in this manner with a view of forcing the commodore to Batavia; but it might be as natural in this light to suppose that they would have been eager to have got him despatched. I therefore rather impute their behaviour to the unparalleled pusillanimity of the nation, and to the awe they are under of the government: for as such a ship as the Centurion, fitted for war only, had never been seen in those parts before, she was the horror of these dastards, and the merchants were in some degree terrified even with the idea of her, and could not think of applying to the viceroy (who is doubtless fond of all opportunities of fleecing them) without representing to themselves the pretences which a hungry and tyrannical magistrate might possibly find, for censuring their intermeddling in so unusual a transaction, in which he might pretend the interest of the state was immediately concerned. However, be this as it may, the commodore was satisfied that nothing was to be done by the interposition of the merchants, as it was on his pressing them to deliver a letter to the viceroy, that they had declared they durst not intermeddle, and had confessed that, notwithstanding all their pretences of serving him, they had not yet taken one step towards it. Mr. Anson

therefore told them that he would proceed to Batavia,
and refit his ship there; but informed them, at the same
time, that this was impossible to be done, unless he was
supplied with a stock of provisions sufficient for his
passage. The merchants, on this, undertook to procure
him provisions, but assured him that it was what they
durst not engage in openly, but proposed to manage it
in a clandestine manner, by putting a quantity of bread,
flour, and other provisions on board the English ships,
which were now ready to sail; and these were to stop
at the mouth of the Typa, where the Centurion's boats
were to receive it. This article, which the merchants
represented as a matter of great favour, being settled,
the commodore, on the 16th of December, returned
from Canton to the ship, seemingly resolved to proceed
to Batavia to refit, as soon as he should get his supplies
of provision on board.

But Mr. Anson (who never intended going to Batavia)
found, on his return to the Centurion, that her mainmast was sprung in two places, and that the leak was
considerably increased; so that, upon the whole, he was
fully satisfied, that though he should lay in a sufficient
stock of provisions, yet it would be impossible for him
to put to sea without refitting: for, if he left the port
with his ship in her present condition, she would be in
the utmost danger of foundering; and therefore, notwithstanding the difficulties he had met with, he resolved at
all events to have her hove down, before he left Macao.
He was fully convinced, by what he had observed at
Canton, that his great caution not to injure the East
India Company's affairs, and the regard he had shown
to the advice of their officers, had occasioned all his

embarrassments. For he now saw clearly that if he had
at first carried his ship into the river of Canton, and had
immediately applied himself to the mandarins, who are
the chief officers of state, instead of employing the
merchants to apply for him; he would, in all probability,
have had all his requests granted, and would have been
soon despatched. He had already lost a month, by the
wrong measures he had been put upon, but he resolved
to lose as little more time as possible; and therefore, the
17th of December, being the next day after his return
from Canton, he wrote a letter to the viceroy of that
place, acquainting him that he was commander-in-chief
of a squadron of his Britannic Majesty's ships of war,
which had been cruising for two years past in the South
Seas against the Spaniards, who were at war with the
king his master; that, in his way back to England, he
had put into the port of Macao, having a considerable
leak in his ship, and being in great want of provisions,
so that it was impossible for him to proceed on his voyage
till his ship was repaired, and he was supplied with the
necessaries he wanted; that he had been at Canton, in
hopes of being admitted to a personal audience of his
excellency; but being a stranger to the customs of the
country, he had not been able to inform himself what
steps were necessary to be taken to procure such an
audience, and therefore was obliged to apply to him in
this manner, to desire his excellency to give order for
his being permitted to employ carpenters and proper
workmen to refit his ship, and to furnish himself with
provisions and stores, thereby to enable him to pursue
his voyage to Great Britain with this monsoon, hoping,
at the same time, that these orders would be issued with

as little delay as possible, lest it might occasion his loss of the season, and he might be prevented from departing till next winter.

This letter was translated into the Chinese language, and the commodore delivered it himself to the hoppo or chief officer of the emperor's customs at Macao, desiring him to forward it to the viceroy of Canton, with as much expedition as he could. The officer at first seemed unwilling to take charge of it, and raised many objections about it, so that Mr. Anson suspected him of being in league with the merchants of Canton, who had always shown a great apprehension of the commodore's having any immediate intercourse with the viceroy or mandarins; and therefore the commodore, with some resentment, took back his letter from the hoppo, and told him he would immediately send an officer with it to Canton in his own boat, and would give him positive orders not to return without an answer from the viceroy. The hoppo, perceiving the commodore to be in earnest, and fearing to be called to an account for his refusal, begged to be entrusted with the letter, and promised to deliver it, and to procure an answer as soon as possible. And now it was soon seen how justly Mr. Anson had at last judged of the proper manner of dealing with the Chinese; for this letter was written but the 17th of December, as hath been already observed; and, on the 19th in the morning a mandarin of the first rank, who was governor of the city of Janson, together with two mandarins of an inferior class, and a great retinue of officers and servants, having with them eighteen half galleys decorated with a greater number of streamers, and furnished with music, and full of men, came to grapnel ahead of the Centurion; whence the mandarin sent a message to the commodore, telling him that he (the mandarin) was ordered, by the viceroy of Canton, to examine the condition of the ship, and desiring the ship's boat might be sent to fetch him on board. The Centurion's boat was immediately despatched, and preparations were made for receiving him; for a hundred of the most sightly of the crew were uniformly dressed in the regimentals of the marines, and were drawn up under arms on the main-deck, against his arrival. When he entered the ship he was saluted by the drums, and what other military music there was on board; and passing by the new-formed guard, he was met by the commodore on the quarter-deck, who conducted him to the great cabin. Here the mandarin explained his commission, declaring that his business was to examine all the particulars mentioned in the commodore's letter to the viceroy, and to confront them with the representation that had been given of them; that he was particularly instructed to inspect the leak, and had for that purpose brought with him two Chinese carpenters; and that for the greater regularity and despatch of his business, he had every head of inquiry separately written down on a sheet of paper, with a void space opposite to it, where he was to insert such information and remarks thereon as he could procure by his own observation.

This mandarin appeared to be a person of very considerable parts, and endowed with more frankness and honesty than is to be found in the generality of the Chinese. After the proper inquiries had been made, particularly about the leak, which the Chinese carpenters reported to be as dangerous as it had been represented,

and consequently that it was impossible for the Centurion
to proceed to sea without being refitted, the mandarin
expressed himself satisfied with the account given in the
commodore's letter.   And this magistrate, as he was
more intelligent than any other person of his nation
that came to our knowledge, so likewise was he more
curious and inquisitive, viewing each part of the ship
with particular attention, and appearing greatly surprised
at the largeness of the lower deck guns, and at the
weight and size of the shot.   The commodore, observing
his astonishment, thought this a proper opportunity to
convince the Chinese of the prudence of granting him a
speedy and ample supply of all he wanted: with this
view he told the mandarin, and those who were with
him, that, besides the demands he made for a general
supply, he had a particular complaint against the proceedings of the custom-house of Macao; that at his first
arrival the Chinese boats had brought on board plenty
of greens, and variety of fresh provisions for daily use,
for which they had always been paid to their full satisfaction, but that the custom-house officers at Macao had
soon forbid them, by which means he was deprived of
those refreshments which were of the utmost consequence to the health of his men, after their long and
sickly voyage; that as they, the mandarins, had informed
themselves of his wants, and were eye-witnesses of the
force and strength of his ship, they might be satisfied it
was not for want of power to supply himself that he
desired the permission of the government to purchase
what provisions he stood in need of; that they must be
convinced that the Centurion alone was capable of
destroying the whole navigation of the port of Canton,

or of any other port in China, without running the least
risk from all the force the Chinese could collect; that it
was true, this was not the manner of proceeding between
nations in friendship with each other; but it was likewise
true, that it was not customary for any nation to permit
the ships of their friends to starve and sink in their ports,
when those friends had money to supply their wants, and
only desired liberty to lay it out; that they must confess he and his people had hitherto behaved with great
modesty and reserve; but that, as his wants were each
day increasing, hunger would at last prove too strong
for any restraint, and necessity was acknowledged in all
countries to be superior to every other law; and therefore it could not be expected that his crew would long
continue to starve in the midst of that plenty to which
their eyes were every day witnesses: to this the commodore added (though perhaps with a less serious air), that
if by the delay of supplying him with provisions his men
should be reduced to the necessity of turning cannibals,
and preying upon their own species, it was easy to be
foreseen that, independent of their friendship to their
comrades, they would, in point of luxury, prefer the
plump well-fed Chinese to their own emaciated shipmates. The first mandarin acquiesced in the justness
of this reasoning, and told the commodore that he
should that night proceed for Canton; that on his
arrival a council of mandarins would be summoned, of
which he himself was a member; and that, by being
employed in the present commission, he was of course
the commodore's advocate; that, as he was fully convinced of the urgency of Mr. Anson's necessity, he did
not doubt but, on his representation, the council would

be of the same opinion; and that all that was demanded
would be amply and speedily granted: and with regard
to the commodore's complaint of the custom-house of
Macao, he undertook to rectify that immediately by his
own authority; for desiring a list to be given him of the
quantity of provisions necessary for the expense of the
ship for a day, he wrote a permit under it, and delivered
it to one of his attendants, directing him to see that
quantity sent on board early every morning; and this
order, from that time forwards, was punctually complied
with.

When this weighty affair was thus in some degree
regulated, the commodore invited him and his two
attendant mandarins to dinner, telling them at the same
time that if his provisions, either in kind or quantity,
were not what they might expect, they must thank themselves for having confined him to so hard an allowance.
One of his dishes was beef, which the Chinese all
dislike, though Mr. Anson was not apprised of it; this
seems to be derived from the Indian superstition, which
for some ages past has made a great progress in China.
However, his guests did not entirely fast; for the three
mandarins completely finished the white part of four
large fowls. But they were extremely embarrassed
with their knives and forks, and were quite incapable
of making use of them: so that, after some fruitless
attempts to help themselves, which were sufficiently
awkward, one of the attendants was obliged to cut their
meat in small pieces for them. But whatever difficulty
they might have in complying with the European
manner of eating, they seemed not to be novices in
drinking. The commodore excused himself in this

part of the entertainment under the pretence of illness;
but there being another gentleman present, of a florid
and jovial complexion, the chief mandarin clapped him
on the shoulder, and told him, by the interpreter, that
certainly he could not plead sickness, and therefore
insisted on his bearing him company; and that
gentleman perceiving, that after they had despatched
four or five bottles of Frontiniac, the mandarin still
continued unruffled, he ordered a bottle of citron water
to be brought up, which the Chinese seemed much to
relish; and this being near finished, they arose from
table, in appearance cool and uninfluenced by what they
had drunk, and the commodore having, according to
custom, made the mandarin a present, they all departed
in the same vessels that brought them.

After their departure the commodore with great
impatience expected the resolution of the council, and
the necessary licenses for his refitment. For it must
be observed, as has already appeared from the preceding
narration, that he could neither purchase stores nor
necessaries with his money, nor did any kind of workmen dare to engage themselves to work for him, without
the permission of the government first obtained. And
in the execution of these particular injunctions the
magistrates never fail of exercising great severity; they,
notwithstanding the fustian eulogiums bestowed upon
them by the catholic missionaries and their European
copiers, being composed of the same fragile materials
with the rest of mankind, and often making use of the
authority of the law, not to suppress crimes, but to
enrich themselves by the pillage of those who commit
them; for capital punishments are rare in China, the

effeminate genius of the nation, and their strong attachment to lucre, disposing them rather to make use of
fines ; and hence arises no inconsiderable profit to those
who compose their tribunals : consequently prohibitions
of all kinds, particularly such as the alluring prospect of
great profit may often tempt the subject to infringe,
cannot but be favourite institutions in such a government. But to return :

Some time before this Captain Saunders took his
passage to England on board a Swedish ship, and was
charged with despatches from the commodore; and
soon after, in the month of December, Captain Mitchel,
Colonel Cracherode, and Mr. Tassel, one of the agent-
victuallers, with his nephew Mr. Charles Harriot,
embarked on board some of our Company's ships ;
and I, having obtained the commodore's leave to return
home, embarked with them. I must observe too (having
omitted it before) that whilst we lay here at Macao, we
were informed by some of the officers of our Indiamen,
that the Severn and Pearl, the two ships of our squadron
which had separated from us off Cape Noir, were safely
arrived at Rio Janeiro on the coast of Brazil. I have
formerly taken notice that, at the time of their separation, we apprehended them to be lost. And there were
many reasons which greatly favoured this suspicion :
for we knew that the Severn in particular was extremely
sickly ; and this was the more obvious to the rest of the
ships, as in the preceding part of the voyage her commander Captain Legge had been remarkable for his
exemplary punctuality in keeping his station, till, for the
last ten days before his separation, his crew was so
diminished and enfeebled, that, with his utmost efforts,

it was not possible for him to maintain his proper position with his wonted exactness. The extraordinary sickness on board him was by many imputed to the ship, which was new, and on that account was believed to be the more unhealthy; but whatever was the cause of it, the Severn was by much the most sickly of the squadron: for before her departure from St. Catherine's she buried more men than any of them, insomuch that the commodore was obliged to recruit her with a number of fresh hands; and, the mortality still continuing on board her, she was supplied with men a second time at sea after our setting sail from St. Julians; and, notwithstanding these different reinforcements, she was at last reduced to the distressed condition I have already mentioned: so that the commodore himself was firmly persuaded she was lost; and therefore it was with great joy we received the news of her and the Pearl's safety, after the strong persuasion, which had so long prevailed amongst us, of their having both perished. But to proceed with the transactions between Mr. Anson and the Chinese.

Notwithstanding the favourable disposition of the mandarin governor of Janson at his leaving Mr. Anson, several days were elapsed before he had any advice from him; and Mr. Anson was privately informed there were great debates in council upon his affair; partly perhaps owing to its being so unusual a case, and in part to the influence, as I suppose, of the intrigues of the French at Canton: for they had a countryman and fast friend residing on the spot who spoke the language very well, and was not unacquainted with the venality of the government, nor with the persons of several of the magistrates, and consequently could not be at a loss for means of traversing the assistance desired by Mr. Anson. And this opposition of the French was not merely the effect of national prejudice or contrariety of political interests, but was in a good measure ·owing to their vanity, a motive of much more weight with the generality of mankind than any attachment to the public service of their community: for, the French pretending their Indiamen to be men-of-war, their officers were apprehensive that any distinction granted to Mr. Anson, on account of his bearing the king's commission, would render them less considerable in the eyes of the Chinese, and would establish a pre-possession at Canton in favour of ships of war, by which they, as trading vessels, would suffer in their import-ance: and I wish the affectation of endeavouring to pass for men-of-war, and the fear of sinking in the estimation of the Chinese, if the Centurion was treated in a different manner from themselves, had been con-fined to the officers of the French ships only. However, notwithstanding all these obstacles, it should seem that the representation of the commodore to the mandarins of the facility with which he could right himself, if justice were denied him, had at last its effect: for, on the 6th of January, in the morning, the governor of Janson, the commodore's advocate, sent down the viceroy of Canton's warrant for the refitment of the Centurion, and for supplying her people with all they wanted; and, the next day, a number of Chinese smiths and carpenters went on board, to agree for all the work by the great. They demanded at first to the amount of a thousand pounds sterling for the necessary repairs of the ship, the boats, and the masts: this the commodore seemed to think an unreasonable sum, and endeavoured to persuade them to work by the day; but that proposal they would not hearken to; so it was at last agreed . that the carpenters should have to the amount of about six hundred pounds for their work; and that the smiths should be paid for their iron-work by weight, allowing them at the rate of three pounds a hundred nearly for the small work, and forty-six shillings for the large.

This being regulated, the commodore exerted himself to get this most important business completed; I mean the heaving down the Centurion, and examining the state of her bottom: for this purpose the first lieutenant was despatched to Canton to hire two country vessels, called in their language junks, one of them being intended to heave down by, and the other to serve as a magazine for the powder and ammunition: at the same time the ground was smoothed on one of the neighbouring islands, and a large tent was pitched for lodging the lumber and provisions, and near a hundred Chinese caulkers were soon set to work on the decks and sides of the ship. But all these preparations, and the getting ready the careening gear, took up a great deal of time; for the Chinese caulkers, though they worked very well, were far from being expeditious; and it was the 26th of January before the junks arrived; and the necessary materials, which were to be purchased at Canton, came down very slowly; partly from the distance of the place, and partly from the delays and backwardness of the Chinese merchants. And in this interval Mr. Anson had the additional perplexity to discover that his foremast was broken asunder above the upper deck partners, and was only kept together by the fishes which had been formerly clapt upon it.

However, the Centurion's people made the most of their time, and exerted themselves the best they could; and as, by clearing the ship, the carpenters were enabled to come at the leak, they took care to secure that effectually whilst the other preparations were going forwards. The leak was found to be below the fifteen foot mark, and was principally occasioned by one of the bolts being worn away and loose in the joining of the stem where it was scarfed.

At last, all things being prepared, they, on the 22nd of February, in the morning, hove out the first course of the Centurion's starboard side, and had the satisfaction to find that her bottom appeared sound and good; and, the next day (having by that time completed the new sheathing of the first course) they righted her again to set up anew the careening rigging, which stretched much. Thus they continued heaving down, and often righting the ship from a suspicion of their careening tackle, till the 3rd of March; when, having completed the paying and sheathing the bottom, which proved to be everywhere very sound; they, for the last time, righted the ship, to their great joy; for not only the fatigue of careening had been considerable, but they had been apprehensive of being attacked by the Spaniards, whilst the ship was thus incapacitated for defence. Nor were their fears altogether groundless; for they learnt afterwards, by a Portuguese vessel, that the Spaniards at Manila had been informed that the Centurion was in the Typa, and intended to careen there; and that there-

upon the governor had summoned his council, and had
proposed to them to endeavour to burn her whilst she
was careening, which was an enterprise which, if properly
conducted, might have put them in great danger: they
were further told that this scheme was not only proposed, but resolved on; and that a captain of a vessel
had actually undertaken to perform the business for
forty thousand dollars, which he was not to receive
unless he succeeded; but the governor pretending that
there was no treasure in the royal chest, and insisting
that the merchants should advance the money, and they
refusing to comply with the demand, the affair was
dropped: perhaps the merchants suspected that the
whole was only a pretext to get forty thousand dollars
from them; and indeed this was affirmed by some who
bore the governor no goodwill, but with what truth it is
difficult to ascertain.

As soon as the Centurion was righted, they took in
her powder, and gunner's stores, and proceeded in
getting in their guns as fast as possible, and then used
their utmost expedition in repairing the foremast, and
in completing the other articles of her refitment. And
being thus employed, they were alarmed, on the 10th
of March, by a Chinese fisherman, who brought them
intelligence that he had been on board a large Spanish
ship off the Grand Ladrone, and that there were two
more in company with her: he added several particulars
to his relation; as that he had brought one of their
officers to Macao; and that, on this, boats went off early
in the morning from Macao to them: and the better to
establish the belief of his veracity, he said he desired no
money, if his information should not prove true. This

was presently believed to be the forementioned expedition from Manila; and the commodore immediately fitted his cannon and small arms in the best manner he could for defence; and having then his pinnace and cutter in the offing, which had been ordered to examine a Portuguese vessel, which was getting under sail, he sent them the advice he had received, and directed them to look out strictly: but no such ships ever appeared, and they were soon satisfied the whole of the story was a fiction; though it was difficult to conceive what reason could induce the fellow to be at such extraordinary pains to impose on them.

It was the beginning of April before they had new-rigged the ship, stowed their provisions and water on board, and had fitted her for the sea; and before this time the Chinese grew very uneasy, and extremely desirous that she should be gone; either not knowing, or pretending not to believe, that this was a point the commodore was as eagerly set on as they could be. On the 3rd of April, two mandarin boats came on board from Macao to urge his departure; and this having been often done before, though there had been no pretence to suspect Mr. Anson of any affected delays, he at this last message answered them in a determined tone, desiring them to give him no further trouble, for he would go when he thought proper, and not before. On this rebuke the Chinese (though it was not in their power to compel him to be gone) immediately prohibited all provisions from being carried on board him, and took such care that their injunctions should be complied with, that from that time forwards nothing could be purchased at any rate whatever.

On the 6th of April, the Centurion weighed from the Typa, and warped to the southward; and, by the 15th, she was got into Macao road, completing her water as she passed along, so that there remained now very few articles more to attend to; and her whole business being finished by the 19th, she, at three in the afternoon of that day, weighed and made sail, and stood to sea.

CHAPTER VIII

From Macao to Cape Espiritu Santo : the taking of the Manila galleon, and returning back again.

THE commodore was now got to sea, with his ship very well refitted, his stores replenished, and an additional stock of provisions on board: his crew too was somewhat reinforced; for he had entered twenty-three men during his stay at Macao, the greatest part of which were Lascars or Indian sailors, and some few Dutch. He gave out at Macao that he was bound to Batavia, and thence to England; and though the westerly monsoon was now set in, when that passage is considered as impracticable, yet, by the confidence he had expressed in the strength of his ship, and the dexterity of his people, he had persuaded not only his own crew, but the people at Macao likewise, that he proposed to try this unusual experiment; so that there were many letters put on board him by the inhabitants of Canton and Macao for their friends at Batavia.

But his real design was of a very different nature; for he knew that instead of one annual ship from Acapulco to Manila there would be this year, in all probability, two; since, by being before Acapulco, he had prevented one of them from putting to sea the preceding season. He therefore resolved to cruise for these returning vessels off Cape Espiritu Santo, on the island of Samal, which is the first land they always make in the Philippine Islands. And as June is generally the month in which they arrive there, he doubted not but he should get to his intended station time enough to intercept them.   It is true they were said to be stout vessels, mounting forty-four guns apiece, and carrying above five hundred hands, and might be expected to return in company; and he himself had but two hundred and twenty-seven hands on board, of which near thirty were boys: but this disproportion of strength did not deter him, as he knew his ship to be much better fitted for a sea-engagement than theirs, and as he had reason to expect that his men would exert themselves in the most extraordinary manner, when they had in view the immense wealth of these Manila galleons.

This project the commodore had resolved on in his own thoughts ever since his leaving the coast of Mexico. And the greatest mortification which he received, from the various delays he had met with in China, was his apprehension, lest he might be thereby so long retarded as to let the galleons escape him.   Indeed, at Macao it was incumbent on him to keep these views extremely secret; for there being a great intercourse and a mutual connexion of interests between that port and Manila, he had reason to fear that if his designs were discovered, intelligence would be immediately sent to Manila, and measures would be taken to prevent the galleons from falling into his hands: but being now at sea, and entirely clear of the coast, he summoned all his people on the quarter-deck, and informed them of his resolution to cruise for the two Manila ships, of whose wealth they were not ignorant. He told them he should choose a station, where he could not fail of meeting with them; and though they were stout ships, and full manned, yet, if his own people behaved with their accustomed spirit, he was certain he should prove too hard for them both, and that one of them at least could not fail of becoming his prize: he further added that many ridiculous tales had been propagated about the strength of the sides of these ships, and their being impenetrable to cannon-shot; that these fictions had been principally invented to palliate the cowardice of those who had formerly engaged them; but he hoped there were none of those present weak enough to give credit to so absurd a story: for his own part, he did assure them upon his word that, whenever he met with them, he would fight them so near that they should find his bullets, instead of being stopped by one of their sides, should go through them both.

This speech of the commodore's was received by his people with great joy: for no sooner had he ended, than they expressed their approbation, according to naval custom, by three strenuous cheers, and all declared their determination to succeed or perish, whenever the opportunity presented itself. And now their hopes, which, since their departure from the coast of Mexico, had entirely subsided, were again revived; and they all persuaded themselves, that, notwithstanding the various casualties and disappointments they had hitherto met with, they should yet be repaid the price of their fatigues, and should at last return home enriched with the spoils of the enemy: for firmly relying on the assurances of the commodore, that they should certainly meet with the vessels, they were all of them too sanguine to doubt a moment of mastering them; so that they considered themselves as having them already in their possession. And this confidence was so universally spread through the whole ship's company, that, the commodore having taken some Chinese sheep to sea with him for his own provision, and one day inquiring of his butcher, why, for some time past, he had seen no mutton at his table, asking him if all the sheep were killed, the butcher very seriously replied that there were indeed two sheep left, but that, if his honour would give him leave, he proposed to keep those for the entertainment of the general of the galleons.

When the Centurion left the port of Macao, she stood for some days to the westward; and, on the 1st of May, they saw part of the island of Formosa; and, standing thence to the southward, they, on the 4th of May, were in the latitude of the Bashee islands, as laid down by Dampier; but they suspected his account of inaccuracy, as they found that he had been considerably mistaken in the latitude of the south end of Formosa: for this reason they kept a good look-out, and about seven in the evening discovered from the mast-head five small islands, which were judged to be the Bashees, and they had afterwards a sight of Botel Tobago Ximo. By this means they had an opportunity of correcting the position of the Bashee islands, which had been hitherto laid down twenty-five leagues too far to the westward: for, by their observations, they esteemed the middle of these islands to be in 21° 4′ north, and to bear from Botel Tobago Ximo S.S.E. twenty leagues distant, that island itself being in 21° 57′ north.

After getting a sight of the Bashee islands, they stood between the S. and S.W. for Cape Espiritu Santo; and, the 20th of May at noon, they first discovered that cape, which about four o'clock they brought to bear S.S.W., about eleven leagues distant. It appeared to be of a moderate height, with several round hummocks on it. As it was known that there were sentinels placed upon this cape to make signals to the Acapulco ship, when she first falls in with the land, the commodore immediately tacked and ordered the top-gallant sails to be taken in, to prevent being discovered; and, this being the station in which it was resolved to cruise for the galleons, they kept the cape between the south and the west, and endeavoured to confine themselves between the latitude of 12° 50′ and 13° 5′, the cape itself lying, by their observations, in 12° 40′ north and in 4° of east longitude from Botel Tobago Ximo.

It was the last of May, by the foreign style, when they arrived off this cape; and, the month of June, by the same style, being that in which the Manila ships are usually expected, the Centurion's people were now waiting each hour with the utmost impatience for the happy crisis which was to balance the account of all their past calamities. As from this time there was but small employment for the crew, the commodore ordered them almost every day to be exercised in the management of the great guns, and in the use of their small arms. This had been his practice, more or less, at all convenient seasons during the whole course of his voyage; and the advantages which he received from it, in his engagement with the galleon, were an ample recompense for all his care and attention. Indeed, it should seem that there

are few particulars of a commander's duty of more importance than this, how much soever it may have been sometimes overlooked or misunderstood : for it will, I suppose,
be confessed that in two ships of war, equal in the
number of their men and guns, the disproportion of
strength, arising from a greater or less dexterity in the
use of their great guns and small arms, is what can
scarcely be balanced by any other circumstances whatever. For, as these are the weapons with which they
are to engage, what greater inequality can there be
betwixt two contending parties, than that one side should
perfectly understand the use of their weapons, and should
have the skill to employ them in the most effectual
manner for the annoyance of their enemy, while the
other side should, by their awkward management of
them, render them rather terrible to themselves, than
mischievous to their antagonists? This seems so plain
and natural a conclusion, that a person unacquainted
with these affairs would suppose the first care of a commander to be the training his people to the use of their
arms.

But human affairs are not always conducted by the
plain dictates of common sense. There are many other
principles which influence our transactions : and there is
one in particular which, though of a very erroneous complexion, is scarcely ever excluded from our most serious
deliberations ; I mean custom, or the practice of those
who have preceded us. This is usually a power too
mighty for reason to grapple with ; and is the most
terrible to those who oppose it, as it has much of superstition in its nature, and pursues all those who question
its authority with unrelenting vehemence. However, in

these later ages of the world, some lucky encroachments
have been made upon its prerogative; and it may reasonably be hoped that the gentlemen of the navy, whose
particular profession hath of late been considerably
improved by a number of new inventions, will of all
others be the readiest to give up those practices which
have nothing to plead but prescription, and will not
suppose that every branch of their business hath already
received all the perfection of which it is capable. Indeed,
it must be owned that, if a dexterity in the use of small
arms, for instance, hath been sometimes less attended to
on board our ships of war, than might have been wished
for, it hath been rather owing to unskilful methods of
teaching it, than to negligence: for the common sailors,
how strongly soever attached to their own prejudices, are
very quick-sighted in finding out the defects of others,
and have ever shown a great contempt for the formalities
practised in the training of land troops to the use of their
arms; but when those who have undertaken to instruct
the seamen have contented themselves with inculcating
only what was useful, and that in the simplest manner,
they have constantly found their people sufficiently
docile, and the success hath even exceeded their expectation. Thus on board Mr. Anson's ship, where they were
only taught the shortest method of loading with cartridges, and were constantly trained to fire at a mark,
which was usually hung at the yard-arm, and where some
little reward was given to the most expert, the whole
crew, by this management, were rendered extremely
skilful, quick in loading, all of them good marksmen,
and some of them most extraordinary ones; so that I
doubt not but, in the use of small arms, they were more

than a match for double their number, who had not been habituated to the same kind of exercise.   But to return :

It was the last of May N.S., as hath been already said, when the Centurion arrived off Cape Espiritu Santo ; and consequently the next day began the month in which the galleons were to be expected.   The commodore therefore made all necessary preparations for receiving them, having hoisted out his long-boat, and lashed her alongside, that the ship might be ready for engaging, if they fell in with the galleons in the night. All this time too he was very solicitous to keep at such a distance from the cape as not to be discovered : but it hath been since learnt that, notwithstanding his care, he was seen from the land ; and advice of him was sent to Manila, where it was at first disbelieved, but on reiterated intelligence (for it seems he was seen more than once) the merchants were alarmed, and the governor was applied to, who undertook (the commerce supplying the necessary sums) to fit out a force consisting of two ships of thirty-two guns, one of twenty guns and two sloops of ten guns, each, to attack the Centurion on her station : and some of these vessels did actually weigh with this view ; but the principal ship not being ready, and the monsoon being against them, the commerce and the governor disagreed, and the enterprise was laid aside. This frequent discovery of the Centurion from the shore was somewhat extraordinary ; for the pitch of the cape is not high, and she usually kept from ten to fifteen leagues distant ; though once indeed, by an indraught of the tide, as was supposed, they found themselves in the morning within seven leagues of the land.

As the month of June advanced, the expectancy and

impatience of the commodore's people each day increased.
And I think no better idea can be given of their great
eagerness on this occasion, than by copying a few paragraphs from the journal of an officer, who was then on
board; as it will, I presume, be a more natural picture
of the full attachment of their thoughts to the business
of their cruise, than can be given by any other means.
The paragraphs I have selected, as they occur in order
of time, are as follow:

"May 31. Exercising our men at their quarters, in
great expectation of meeting with the galleons very soon;
this being the eleventh of June their style."

"June 3. Keeping in our stations, and looking out
for the galleons."

"June 5. Begin now to be in great expectation, this
being the middle of June their style."

"June 11. Begin to grow impatient at not seeing the
galleons."

"June 13. The wind having blown fresh easterly for
the forty-eight hours past, gives us great expectations of
seeing the galleons soon."

"June 15. Cruising on and off, and looking out
strictly."

"June 19. This being the last day of June N.S., the
galleons, if they arrive at all, must appear soon."

From these samples it is sufficiently evident how
completely the treasure of the galleons had engrossed
their imagination, and how anxiously they passed the
latter part of their cruise, when the certainty of the
arrival of these vessels was dwindled down to probability
only, and that probability became each hour more and

more doubtful. However, on the 20th of June O.S.,
being just a month from their arrival on their station,
they were relieved from this state of uncertainty; when,
at sunrise, they discovered a sail from the mast-head, in
the S.E. quarter. On this, a general joy spread through
the whole ship; for they had no doubt but this was one
of the galleons, and they expected soon to see the other.
The commodore instantly stood towards her, and at half
an hour after seven they were near enough to see her
from the Centurion's deck; at which time the galleon
fired a gun, and took in her top-gallant sails, which was
supposed to be a signal to her consort, to hasten her up;
and therefore the Centurion fired a gun to leeward, to
amuse her. The commodore was surprised to find that
in all this time the galleon did not change her course,
but continued to bear down upon him; for he hardly
believed, what afterwards appeared to be the case, that
she knew his ship to be the Centurion, and resolved to
fight him.

About noon the commodore was little more than a
league distant from the galleon, and could fetch her
wake, so that she could not now escape; and, no second
ship appearing, it was concluded that she had been
separated from her consort. Soon after, the galleon
hauled up her foresail, and brought-to under topsails,
with her head to the northward, hoisting Spanish colours,
and having the standard of Spain flying at the top-gallant
mast-head. Mr. Anson, in the meantime, had prepared
all things for an engagement on board the Centurion,
and had taken all possible care, both for the most
effectual exertion of his small strength, and for the avoiding the confusion and tumult, too frequent in actions of

this kind. He picked out about thirty of his choicest hands and best marksmen, whom he distributed into his tops, and who fully answered his expectation, by the signal services they performed. As he had not hands enough remaining to quarter a sufficient number to each great gun, in the customary manner, he therefore, on his lower tier, fixed only two men to each gun, who were to be solely employed in loading it, whilst the rest of his people were divided into different gangs of ten and twelve men each, which were constantly moving about the decks, to run out and fire such guns as were loaded. By this management he was enabled to make use of all his guns; and, instead of firing broadsides with intervals between them, he kept up a constant fire without intermission, whence he doubted not to procure very signal advantages; for it is common with the Spaniards to fall down upon the decks when they see a broadside preparing, and to continue in that posture till it is given; after which they rise again, and, presuming the danger to be some time over, work their guns, and fire with great briskness, till another broadside is ready: but the firing gun by gun, in the manner directed by the commodore, rendered this practice of theirs impossible.

The Centurion being thus prepared, and nearing the galleon apace, there happened, a little after noon, several squalls of wind and rain, which often obscured the galleon from their sight; but whenever it cleared up, they observed her resolutely lying-to; and, towards one o'clock, the Centurion hoisted her broad pendant and colours, she being then within gun-shot of the enemy. And the commodore observing the Spaniards to have neglected clearing their ship till that time, as he then

saw them throwing overboard cattle and lumber, he
gave orders to fire upon them with the chase-guns, to
embarrass them in their work, and prevent them from
completing it, though his general directions had been
not to engage till they were within pistol-shot. The
galleon returned the fire with two of her stern-chasers;
and the Centurion getting her spritsail-yard fore and aft,
that if necessary she might be ready for boarding; the
Spaniards in a bravado rigged their spritsail-yard fore
and aft likewise. Soon after, the Centurion came abreast
of the enemy within pistol-shot, keeping to the leeward
with a view of preventing them from putting before the
wind, and gaining the port of Jalapay, from which they
were about seven leagues distant. And now the engagement began in earnest, and, for the first half hour, Mr.
Anson over-reached the galleon, and lay on her bow;
where, by the great wideness of his ports, he could traverse
almost all his guns upon the enemy, whilst the galleon
could only bring a part of hers to bear. Immediately
on the commencement of the action, the mats, with
which the galleon had stuffed her netting, took fire, and
burnt violently, blazing up half as high as the mizen-top.
This accident (supposed to be caused by the Centurion's
wads) threw the enemy into great confusion, and at the
same time alarmed the commodore, for he feared lest
the galleon should be burnt, and lest he himself too
might suffer by her driving on board him: but the
Spaniards at last freed themselves from the fire, by
cutting away the netting, and tumbling the whole mass
which was in flames, into the sea. But still the Centurion
kept her first advantageous position, firing her cannon
with great regularity and briskness, whilst at the same

time the galleon's decks lay open to her top-men, who, having at their first volley driven the Spaniards from their tops, made prodigious havoc with their small arms, killing or wounding every officer but one that ever appeared on the quarter-deck, and wounding in particular the general of the galleon himself. And though the Centurion, after the first half hour, lost her original situation, and was close alongside the galleon, and the enemy continued to fire briskly for near an hour longer, yet at last the commodore's grape-shot swept their decks so effectually, and the number of their slain and wounded was so considerable, that they began to fall into great disorder, especially as the general, who was the life of the action, was no longer capable of exerting himself. Their embarrassment was visible from on board the commodore. For the ships were so near, that some of the Spanish officers were seen running about with great assiduity, to prevent the desertion of their men from their quarters: but all their endeavours were in vain; for after having, as a last effort, fired five or six guns with more judgment than usual, they gave up the contest; and, the galleon's colours being singed off the ensign-staff in the beginning of the engagement, she struck the standard at her main-top-gallant mast-head, the person who was employed to do it having been in imminent peril of being killed, had not the commodore, who perceived what he was about, given express orders to his people to desist from firing.

Thus was the Centurion possessed of this rich prize, amounting in value to near a million and a half of dollars. She was called the Nostra Signora de Cabadonga, and was commanded by the general Don Jeronimo de

Montero, a Portuguese by birth, and the most approved officer for skill and courage of any employed in that service. The galleon was much larger than the Centurion, had five hundred and fifty men and thirty-six guns mounted for action, besides twenty-eight pidreroes in her gunwale, quarters, and tops, each of which carried a four-pound ball. She was very well furnished with small arms, and was particularly provided against boarding, both by her close quarters, and by a strong net-work of two inch rope, which was laced over her waist, and was defended by half pikes. She had sixty-seven killed in the action, and eighty-four wounded, whilst the Centurion had only two killed, and a lieutenant and sixteen wounded, all of whom, but one, recovered : of so little consequence are the most destructive arms in untutored and unpractised hands !

The treasure thus taken by the Centurion having been for at least eighteen months the great object of their hopes, it is impossible to describe the transport on board, when, after all their reiterated disappointments, they at last saw their wishes accomplished. But their joy was near being suddenly damped by a most tremendous incident : for no sooner had the galleon struck, than one of the lieutenants coming to Mr. Anson to congratulate him on his prize, whispered him at the same time that the Centurion was dangerously on fire near the powder-room. The commodore received this dreadful news without any apparent emotion, and, taking care not to alarm his people, gave the necessary orders for extinguishing it, which was happily done in a short time, though its appearance at first was extremely terrible. It seems some cartridges had been blown up by accident between decks, whereby a quantity of oakum in the after-hatchway, near the after powder-room, was set on fire; and the great smother and smoke of the oakum occasioned the apprehension of a more extended and mischievous fire. At the same instant, too, the galleon fell on board the Centurion on the starboard quarter, but she was cleared without doing or receiving any considerable damage.

The commodore made his first lieutenant, Mr. Saumarez, captain of this prize, appointing her a post-ship in His Majesty's service. Captain Saumarez, before night, sent on board the Centurion all the Spanish prisoners, but such as were thought the most proper to be retained to assist in navigating the galleon. And now the commodore learnt, from some of these prisoners, that the other ship, which he had kept in the port of Acapulco the preceding year, instead of returning in company with the present prize as was expected, had set sail from Acapulco alone much sooner than usual, and had, in all probability, got into the port of Manila long before the Centurion arrived off Espiritu Santo; so that Mr. Anson, notwithstanding his present success, had great reason to regret his loss of time at Macao, which prevented him from taking two rich prizes instead of one.

The commodore, when the action was ended, resolved to make the best of his way with his prize for the river of Canton, being in the meantime fully employed in securing his prisoners, and in removing the treasure from on board the galleon into the Centurion. The last of these operations was too important to be postponed; for, as the navigation to Canton was through

seas but little known, and where, from the season of the
year, much bad weather might be expected, it was of
great consequence that the treasure should be sent on
board the Centurion, which ship, by the presence of the
commander-in-chief, the greater number of her hands,
and her other advantages, was doubtless much safer
against all the casualties of winds and seas than the
galleon : and the securing the prisoners was a matter of
still more consequence, as not only the possession of
the treasure, but the lives of the captors, depended
thereon. This was indeed an article which gave the
commodore much trouble and disquietude; for they
were above double the number of his own people; and
some of them, when they were brought on board the
Centurion, and had observed how slenderly she was
manned, and the large proportion which the striplings
bore to the rest, could not help expressing themselves
with great indignation, to be thus beaten by a handful
of boys. The method which was taken to hinder them
from rising, was by placing all but the officers and the
wounded in the hold, where, to give them as much air
as possible, two hatchways were left open; but then (to
avoid all danger whilst the Centurion's people should
be employed upon the deck) there was a square partition
of thick planks, made in the shape of a funnel, which
enclosed each hatchway on the lower deck, and reached
to that directly over it on the upper deck; these funnels
served to communicate the air to the hold better than
could have been done without them; and, at the same
time, added greatly to the security of the ship; for they
being seven or eight feet high, it would have been
extremely difficult for the Spaniards to have clambered

up; and still to augment that difficulty, four swivel-guns,
loaded with musket-bullets, were planted at the mouth
of each funnel, and a sentinel with a lighted match
constantly attended, prepared to fire into the hold
amongst them, in case of any disturbance. Their
officers, who amounted to seventeen or eighteen, were
all lodged in the first lieutenant's cabin, under a constant
guard of six men; and the general, as he was wounded,
lay in the commodore's cabin with a sentinel always
with him; and they were all informed that any violence
or disturbance would be punished with instant death.
And that the Centurion's people might be at all times
prepared, if, notwithstanding these regulations, any
tumult should arise, the small arms were constantly kept
loaded in a proper place, whilst all the men went armed
with cutlasses and pistols; and no officer ever pulled off
his clothes, and when he slept had always his arms lying
ready by him.

These measures were obviously necessary, considering the hazards to which the commodore and his people
would have been exposed, had they been less careful.
Indeed, the sufferings of the poor prisoners, though
impossible to be alleviated, were much to be com-
miserated; for the weather was extremely hot, the
stench of the hold loathsome, beyond all conception,
and their allowance of water but just sufficient to keep
them alive, it not being practicable to spare them more
than at the rate of a pint a day for each, the crew themselves having only an allowance of a pint and a half.
All this considered, it was wonderful that not a man of
them died during their long confinement, except three
of the wounded, who died the same night they were

taken : though it must be confessed that the greatest
part of them were strangely metamorphosed by the heat
of the hold; for when they were first taken, they were
sightly, robust fellows; but when, after above a month's
imprisonment, they were discharged in the river of
Canton, they were reduced to mere skeletons; and their
air and looks corresponded much more to the conception
formed of ghosts and spectres, than to the figure and
appearance of real men.

Thus employed in securing the treasure and the
prisoners, the commodore, as hath been said, stood for
the river of Canton; and, on the 30th of June, at six
in the evening, got sight of Cape Delangano, which
then bore west ten leagues distant; and the next day
he made the Bashee islands, and the wind being so far
to the northward, that it was difficult to weather them,
it was resolved to stand through between Grafton and
Monmouth islands, where the passage seemed to be
clear; but in getting through, the sea had a very
dangerous aspect, for it rippled and foamed, as if it had
been full of breakers, which was still more terrible, as it
was then night. But the ships got through very safe
(the prize always keeping ahead), and it was found that
the appearance which had alarmed them had been
occasioned only by a strong tide. I must here observe
that though the Bashee islands are usually reckoned to
be no more than five, yet there are many more lying
about them to the westward, which, as the channels
amongst them are not at all known, makes it advisable
for ships rather to pass to the northward or southward,
than through them; and indeed the commodore proposed to have gone to the northward, between them and

Formosa, had it been possible for him to have weathered them. From hence the Centurion steering the proper course for the river of Canton, she, on the 8th of July, discovered the island of Supata, the westernmost of the Lema islands, being the double-peaked rock, formerly referred to. This island of Supata they made to be a hundred and thirty-nine leagues distant from Grafton's island, and to bear from it north 82° 37' west: and, on the 11th, having taken on board two Chinese pilots, one for the Centurion, and the other for the prize, they came to an anchor off the city of Macao.

By this time the particulars of the cargo of the galleon were well ascertained, and it was found that she had on board 1,313,843 pieces of eight, and 35,682 oz. of virgin silver, besides some cochineal, and a few other commodities, which, however, were but of small account in comparison of the specie. And this being the commodore's last prize, it hence appears that all the treasure taken by the Centurion was not much short of £400,000 independent of the ships and merchandise, which she either burnt or destroyed, and which, by the most reasonable estimation, could not amount to so little as £600,000 more: so that the whole loss of the enemy, by our squadron, did doubtless exceed a million sterling. To which, if there be added the great expense of the court of Spain, in fitting out Pizarro, and in paying the additional charges in America, incurred on our account, together with the loss of their men-of-war, the total of all these articles will be a most exorbitant sum, and is the strongest conviction of the utility of this expedition, which, with all its numerous disadvantages, did yet prove so extremely prejudicial to the enemy.

I shall only add, that there were taken on board the galleon several draughts and journals, from some of which many of the particulars recited in the 10th chapter of the second book are collected. Among the rest there was found a chart of all the ocean, between the Philippines and the coast of Mexico, which was what was made use of by the galleon in her own navigation.

CHAPTER IX

Transactions in the river of Canton.

THE commodore, having taken pilots on board, proceeded with his prize for the river of Canton; and, on
the 14th of July, came to an anchor short of the Bocca
Tigris, which is a narrow passage forming the mouth
of that river: this entrance he proposed to stand through
the next day, and to run up as far as Tiger Island, which
is a very safe road, secured from all winds. But whilst
the Centurion and her prize were thus at anchor, a boat
with an officer came off from the mandarin, commanding
the forts at Bocca Tigris to examine what the ships
were, and whence they came. Mr. Anson informed the
officer that his ship was a ship of war, belonging to the
king of Great Britain; and that the other in company
with him was a prize he had taken; that he was going
into Canton river to shelter himself against the hurricanes
which were then coming on; and that, as soon as the
monsoon shifted, he should proceed for England. The
officer then desired an account of what men, guns, and
ammunition were on board, a list of all which he said
was to be sent to the government of Canton. But when
these articles were repeated to him, particularly when

he was told that there were in the Centurion four
hundred firelocks, and between three and four hundred
barrels of powder, he shrugged up his shoulders, and
seemed to be terrified with the bare recital, saying, that
no ships ever came into Canton river armed in that
manner; adding, that he durst not set down the whole
of this force, lest it should too much alarm the regency.
After he had finished his inquiries, and was preparing
to depart, he desired to leave two custom-house officers
behind him; on which the commodore told him, that
though as a man-of-war he was prohibited from trading,
and had nothing to do with customs or duties of any
kind, yet, for the satisfaction of the Chinese, he would
permit two of their people to be left on board, who
might themselves be witnesses how punctually he should
comply with his instructions. The officer seemed
amazed when Mr. Anson mentioned being exempted
from all duties, and told him that the emperor's duty
must be paid by all ships that came into his ports: and
it is supposed that, on this occasion, private directions
were given by him to the Chinese pilot, not to carry the
commodore through the Bocca Tigris; which makes it
necessary, more particularly, to describe that entrance.

The Bocca Tigris is a narrow passage, little more than
musket-shot over, formed by two points of land, on each
of which there is a fort, that on the starboard side being
a battery on the water's edge, with eighteen embrasures,
but where there were no more than twelve iron cannon
mounted, seeming to be four or six pounders; the fort
on the larboard side is a large castle, resembling those
old buildings which here in England we often find
distinguished by that name; it is situated on a high

rock, and did not appear to be furnished with more than eight or ten cannon, none of which were supposed to exceed six-pounders. These are the defences which secure the river of Canton; and which the Chinese (extremely defective in all military skill) have imagined were sufficient to prevent any enemy from forcing his way through.

But it is obvious, from the description of these forts, that they could have given no obstruction to Mr. Anson's passage, even if they had been well supplied with gunners and stores; and therefore, though the pilot, after the Chinese officer had been on board, refused at first to take charge of the ship till he had leave from the forts, yet as it was necessary to get through without any delay, for fear of the bad weather which was hourly expected, the commodore weighed on the 15th, and ordered the pilot to carry him by the forts, threatening him that, if the ship ran aground, he would instantly hang him up at the yard-arm. The pilot, awed by these threats, carried the ship through safely, the forts not attempting to dispute the passage. Indeed the poor pilot did not escape the resentment of his countrymen, for when he came on shore, he was seized and sent to prison, and was rigorously disciplined with the bamboo. However, he found means to get at Mr. Anson afterwards, to desire of him some recompense for the chastisement he had undergone, and of which he then carried very significant marks about him; and Mr. Anson, in com- miseration of his sufferings, gave him such a sum of money, as would at any time have enticed a Chinese to have undergone a dozen bastinadings.

Nor was the pilot the only person that suffered on

this occasion; for the commodore soon after seeing some royal junks pass by him from Bocca Tigris towards Canton, he learnt, on inquiry, that the mandarin commanding the forts was a prisoner on board them; that he was already turned out, and was now carrying to Canton, where it was expected he would be severely punished for having permitted the ships to pass; and the commodore urging the unreasonableness of this procedure, from the inability of the forts to have done otherwise, explaining to the Chinese the great superiority his ships would have had over the forts, by the number and size of their guns, the Chinese seemed to acquiesce in his reasoning, and allowed that their forts could not have stopped him; but they still asserted that the mandarin would infallibly suffer for not having done what all his judges were convinced was impossible. To such indefensible absurdities are those obliged to submit, who think themselves concerned to support their authority, when the necessary force is wanting. But to return:

On the 16th of July the commodore sent his second lieutenant to Canton, with a letter to the viceroy, informing him of the reason of the Centurion's putting into that port; and that the commodore himself soon proposed to repair to Canton, to pay a visit to the viceroy. The lieutenant was very civilly received, and was promised that an answer should be sent to the commodore the next day. In the meantime Mr. Anson gave leave to several of the officers of the galleon to go to Canton, they engaging their parole to return in two days. When these prisoners got to Canton, the regency sent for them, and examined them, inquiring particularly by what means they had fallen into Mr. Anson's power. And on this occasion the prisoners were honest enough to declare that, as the kings of Great Britain and of Spain were at war, they had proposed to themselves the taking of the Centurion, and had bore down upon her with that view, but that the event had been contrary to their hopes: however, they acknowledged that they had been treated by the commodore much better than they believed they should have treated him, had he fallen into their hands. This confession from an enemy had great weight with the Chinese, who, till then, though they had revered the commodore's power, had yet suspected his morals, and had considered him rather as a lawless freebooter than as one commissioned by the state for the revenge of public injuries. But they now changed their opinion, and regarded him as a more important person; to which perhaps the vast treasure of his prize might not a little contribute; the acquisition of wealth being a matter greatly adapted to the estimation and reverence of the Chinese nation.

In this examination of the Spanish prisoners, though the Chinese had no reason in the main to doubt of the account which was given them, yet there were two circumstances which appeared to them so singular as to deserve a more ample explanation; one of them was the great disproportion of men between the Centurion and the galleon; the other was the humanity, with which the people of the galleon were treated after they were taken. The mandarins therefore asked the Spaniards how they came to be overpowered by so inferior a force; and how it happened, since the two nations were at war, that they were not put to death when they came into the hands of the English. To the first of these inquiries the Spaniards replied, that though they had more hands than the Centurion, yet she being intended solely for war, had a great superiority in the size of her guns, and in many other articles, over the galleon, which was a vessel fitted out principally for traffic: and as to the second question, they told the Chinese that, amongst the nations of Europe, it was not customary to put to death those who submitted; though they readily owned that the commodore, from the natural bias of his temper, had treated both them and their countrymen, who had formerly been in his power, with very unusual courtesy, much beyond what they could have expected, or than was required by the customs established between nations at war with each other. These replies fully satisfied the Chinese, and at the same time wrought very powerfully in the commodore's favour.

On the 20th of July, in the morning, three mandarins, with a great number of boats, and a vast retinue, came on board the Centurion, and delivered to the commodore the viceroy of Canton's order for a daily supply of provisions, and for pilots to carry the ships up the river as far as the second bar; and at the same time they delivered him a message from the viceroy, in answer to the letter sent to Canton. The substance of the message was, that the viceroy desired to be excused from receiving the commodore's visit, during the then excessive hot weather; because the assembling the mandarins and soldiers, necessary to that ceremony, would prove extremely inconvenient and fatiguing; but that in September, when the weather would be more temperate, he should be glad to see both the commodore himself, and the English captain of the other ship that was with him. As

Mr Anson knew that an express had been despatched to the court at Pekin, with an account of the Centurion and her prize being arrived in the river of Canton, he had no doubt but the principal motive for putting off this visit was, that the regency at Canton might gain time to receive the emperor's instructions about their behaviour in this unusual affair.

When the mandarins had delivered their message, they began to talk to the commodore about the duties to be paid by his ships; but he immediately told them that he would never submit to any demand of that kind; that as he neither brought any merchandise thither, nor intended to carry any away, he could not be reasonably deemed to be within the meaning of the emperor's orders, which were doubtless calculated for trading vessels only; adding, that no duties were ever demanded of men-of-war, by nations accustomed to their reception, and that his master's orders expressly forbade him from paying any acknowledgment for his ships anchoring in any port whatever.

The mandarins being thus cut short on the subject of the duty, they said they had another matter to mention, which was the only remaining one they had in charge; this was a request to the commodore, that he would release the prisoners he had taken on board the galleon; for that the viceroy of Canton apprehended the emperor, his master, might be displeased, if he should be informed that persons, who were his allies, and carried on a great commerce with his subjects, were under confinement in his dominions. Mr. Anson was himself extremely desirous to get rid of the Spaniards, having, on his first arrival, sent about a hundred of them to Macao, and those who remained, which were near four hundred more, were on many accounts, a great incumbrance to him. However, to inhance the favour, he at first raised some difficulties; but permitting himself to be prevailed on, he at last told the mandarins, that to show his readiness to oblige the viceroy, he would release the prisoners, whenever they, the Chinese, would send boats to fetch them off. This matter being thus adjusted, the mandarins departed; and, on the 28th of July, two Chinese junks were sent from Canton, to take on board the prisoners, and to carry them to Macaò. And the commodore, agreeably to his promise, dismissed them all, and ordered his purser to send with them eight days' provision for their subsistence, during their sailing down the river; this being despatched, the Centurion and her prize came to her moorings, about the second bar, where they proposed to continue till the monsoon shifted.

Though the ships, in consequence of the viceroy's permit, found no difficulty in purchasing provisions for their daily consumption, yet it was impossible for the commodore to proceed to England, without laying in a large quantity both of provisions and stores for his use, during the voyage: the procuring this supply was attended with much embarrassment; for there were people at Canton who had undertaken to furnish him with biscuit, and whatever else he wanted; and his linguist, towards the middle of September, had assured him, from day to day, that all was ready, and would be sent on board him immediately. But a fortnight being elapsed, and nothing being brought, the commodore sent to Canton to inquire more particularly into the reasons of this disappointment: and he had soon the vexation to be informed that the whole was an illusion; that no order had been procured from the viceroy to furnish him with his sea-stores, as had been pretended; that there was no biscuit baked, nor any one of the articles in readiness, which had been promised him; nor did it appear that the contractors had taken the least step to comply with their agreement. This was most disagreeable news, and made it suspected, that the furnishing the Centurion for her return to Great Britain might prove a more troublesome matter than had been hitherto imagined; especially, too, as the month of September was nearly elapsed, without Mr. Anson's having received any message from the viceroy of Canton.

It were endless to recount all the artifices, extortions, and frauds which were practised on the commodore and his people, by this interested race. The method of buying all things in China being by weight, the tricks made use of by the Chinese to increase the weight of the provision they sold to the Centurion, were almost incredible. One time a large quantity of fowls and ducks being bought for the ship's use, the greatest part of them presently died. This alarmed the people on board with the apprehension that they had been killed by poison; but on examination it appeared that it was only owing to their being crammed with stones and gravel to increase their weight, the quantity thus forced into most of the ducks being found to amount to ten ounces in each. The hogs too, which were bought ready killed of the Chinese butchers, had water injected into them for the same purpose; so that a carcass, hung up all night for the water to drain from it, has lost above a stone of its weight; and when, to avoid this cheat, the hogs were bought alive, it was found that the Chinese gave them salt to increase their thirst, and, having by this means excited them to drink great quantities of water, they sold the tortured animals in this inflated state. When the commodore first put to sea from Macao, they practised an artifice of another kind; for, as the Chinese never object to the eating of any food that dies of itself, they took care, by some secret practices, that great part of his live sea-store should die in a short time after it was put on board, hoping to make a second profit of the dead carcases which they expected would be thrown overboard; and two-thirds of the hogs dying before the Centurion was out of sight of land, many of the Chinese boats followed her only to pick up the carrion. These instances may serve as a specimen of the manners of this celebrated nation, which is often recommended to the rest of the world as a pattern of all kinds of laudable qualities. But to return:

The commodore, towards the end of September, having found out (as has been said) that those who had contracted to supply him with sea-provisions and stores had deceived him, and that the viceroy had not sent to him according to his promise, he saw it would be impossible for him to surmount the embarrassment he was under without going himself to Canton, and visiting the viceroy; and therefore, on the 27th of September, he sent a message to the mandarin who attended the Centurion, to inform him that he, the commodore, intended, on the first of October, to proceed in his boat to Canton; adding, that the day after he got there, he should notify his arrival to the viceroy, and should desire him to fix a time for his audience; to which the mandarin returned no other answer, than that he would acquaint the viceroy with the commodore's intentions.

In the meantime all things were prepared for this expedition; and the boat's crew in particular, which Mr. Anson proposed to take with him, were clothed in a uniform dress, resembling that of the watermen on the Thames; they were in number eighteen and a coxswain; they had scarlet jackets and blue silk waistcoats, the whole trimmed with silver buttons, and with silver badges on their jackets and caps. As it was apprehended, and even asserted, that the payment of the customary duties for the Centurion and her prize would be demanded by the regency of Canton, and would be insisted on previous to the granting a permission for victualling the ship for her future voyage; the commodore, who was resolved never to establish so dishonourable a precedent, took all possible precaution to prevent the Chinese from facilitating the success of their unreasonable pretentions by having him in their power at Canton: and therefore, for the security of his ship, and the great treasure on board her, he appointed his first lieutenant, Mr. Brett, to be captain of the Centurion under him, giving him proper instructions for his conduct; directing him, particularly, if he, the commodore, should be detained at Canton on account of the duties in dispute, to take out the men from the Centurion's prize, and to destroy her; and then to proceed down the river through the Bocca Tigris, with the Centurion alone, and to remain without that entrance till he received further orders from Mr. Anson.

These necessary steps being taken, which were not unknown to the Chinese, it should seem as if their deliberations were in some sort embarrassed thereby. It is reasonable to imagine that they were in general very desirous of getting the duties to be paid them; not perhaps solely in consideration of the amount of those dues, but to keep up their reputation for address and subtlety, and to avoid the imputation of receding from claims on which they had already so frequently insisted. However, as they now foresaw that they had no other method of succeeding than by violence, and that even against this the commodore was prepared, they were at last disposed, I conceive, to let the affair drop, rather than entangle themselves in a hostile measure, which they found would only expose them to the risk of having the whole navigation of their port destroyed, without any certain prospect of gaining their favourite point thereby.

However, though there is reason to imagine that these were their thoughts at that time, yet they could not depart at once from the evasive conduct to which they had hitherto adhered. For when the commodore, on the morning of the first of October, was preparing to set out for Canton, his linguist came to him from the mandarin who attended his ship, to tell him that a letter had been received from the viceroy of Canton, desiring the commodore to put off his going thither for two or three days: but in the afternoon of the same day another linguist came on board, who, with much seeming fright, told Mr. Anson that the viceroy had expected him up that day, that the council was assembled, and the troops had been under arms to receive him; and that the viceroy was highly offended at the disappointment, and had sent the commodore's linguist to prison chained, supposing that the whole had been owing to the linguist's negligence. This plausible tale gave the commodore great concern, and made him apprehend that there was some treachery designed him, which he could not yet fathom; and though it afterwards appeared that the whole was a fiction, not one article of it having the least foundation, yet (for reasons best known to themselves) this falsehood was so well supported by the artifices of the Chinese merchants at Canton, that, three days afterwards, the commodore received a letter signed by all the supercargoes of the English ships then at that place, expressing their great uneasiness at what had happened, and intimating their fears that some insult would be offered to his boat if he came thither before the viceroy was fully satisfied about the mistake. To this letter Mr. Anson replied, that he did not believe there had been any mistake; but was persuaded it was a forgery of the Chinese to prevent his visiting the viceroy; that therefore he would certainly come up to Canton on the 13th of October, confident that the Chinese would not dare to offer him an insult, as well knowing it would be properly returned.

On the 13th of October, the commodore continuing firm to his resolution, all the supercargoes of the English, Danish, and Swedish ships came on board the Centurion, to accompany him to Canton, for which place he set out in his barge the same day, attended by his own boats, and by those of the trading ships, which on this occasion came to form his retinue; and as he passed by Wampo, where the European vessels lay, he was saluted by all of them but the French, and in the evening he arrived safely at Canton. His reception at that city, and the most material transactions from henceforward, till his arrival in Great Britain, shall be the subject of the ensuing chapter.

CHAPTER X

Proceedings at the city of Canton, and the return of the
Centurion to England.

WHEN the commodore arrived at Canton he was visited
by the principal Chinese merchants, who affected to
appear very much pleased that he had met with no
obstruction in getting thither, and who thence pretended
to conclude that the viceroy was satisfied about the
former mistake, the reality of which they still insisted on :
they added, that as soon as the viceroy should be informed that Mr. Anson was at Canton (which they
promised should be done the next morning), they were
persuaded a day would be immediately appointed for
the visit, which was the principal business that had
brought the commodore thither.

The next day the merchants returned to Mr. Anson,
and told him that the viceroy was then so fully employed
in preparing his despatches for Pekin, that there was no
getting admittance to him for some days ; but that they
had engaged one of the officers of his court to give them
information, as soon as he should be at leisure, when
they proposed to notify Mr. Anson's arrival, and to
endeavour to fix the day of audience. The commodore

was by this time too well acquainted with their artifices not to perceive that this was a falsehood; and had he consulted only his own judgment, he would have applied directly to the viceroy by other hands: but the Chinese merchants had so far prepossessed the supercargoes of our ships with chimerical fears, that they (the super-cargoes) were extremely apprehensive of being embroiled with the government, and of suffering in their interest, if those measures were taken, which appeared to Mr. Anson at that time to be the most prudential: and therefore, lest the malice and double-dealing of the Chinese might have given rise to some sinister incident, which would be afterwards laid at his door, he resolved to continue passive, as long as it should appear that he lost no time, by thus suspending his own opinion. With this view, he promised not to take any immediate step himself for getting admittance to the viceroy, provided the Chinese, with whom he contracted for provisions, would let him see that his bread was baked, his meat salted, and his stores prepared with the utmost despatch; but if, by the time when all was in readiness to be shipped off (which it was supposed would be in about forty days), the merchants should not have procured the viceroy's per-mission, then the commodore proposed to apply for it himself. These were the terms Mr. Anson thought proper to offer, to quiet the uneasiness of the supercargoes; and, notwithstanding the apparent equity of the conditions, many difficulties and objections were urged; nor would the Chinese agree to them, till the commodore had con-sented to pay for every article he bespoke before it was put in hand. However, at last, the contract being passed, it was some satisfaction to the commodore to be certain

that his preparations were now going on, and being himself on the spot, he took care to hasten them as much
as possible.

During this interval, in which the stores and provisions
were getting ready, the merchants continually entertained
Mr. Anson with accounts of their various endeavours to
get a license from the viceroy, and their frequent disappointments; which to him was now a matter of
amusement, as he was fully satisfied there was not one
word of truth in anything they said.   But when all was
completed, and wanted only to be shipped, which was
about the 24th of November, at which time too the N.E.
monsoon was set in, he then resolved to apply himself
to the viceroy to demand an audience, as he was
persuaded that, without this ceremony, the procuring a
permission to send his stores on board would meet with
great difficulty.   On the 24th of November, therefore,
Mr. Anson sent one of his officers to the mandarin, who
commanded the guard of the principal gate of the city of
Canton, with a letter directed to the viceroy.   When this
letter was delivered to the mandarin, he received the
officer who brought it very civilly, and took down the
contents of it in Chinese, and promised that the viceroy
should be immediately acquainted with it; but told the
officer it was not necessary for him to wait for an answer,
because a message would be sent to the commodore
himself.

On this occasion Mr. Anson had been under great
difficulties about a proper interpreter to send with his
officer, as he was well aware that none of the Chinese,
usually employed as linguists, could be relied on: but
he at last prevailed with Mr. Flint, an English gentleman

belonging to the factory, who spoke Chinese perfectly well, to accompany his officer. This person, who, upon this occasion and many others, was of singular service to the commodore, had been left at Canton when a youth, by the late Captain Rigby. The leaving him there to learn the Chinese language was a step taken by that captain, merely from his own persuasion of the great advantages which the East India Company might one day receive from an English interpreter; and though the utility of this measure has greatly exceeded all that was expected from it, yet I have not heard that it has been to this day imitated: but we imprudently choose (except in this single instance) to carry on the vast transactions of the port of Canton, either by the ridiculous jargon of broken English which some few of the Chinese have learnt, or by the suspected interpretation of the linguists of other nations.

Two days after the sending the above-mentioned letter, a fire broke out in the suburbs of Canton. On the first alarm, Mr. Anson went thither with his officers, and his boat's crew, to assist the Chinese. When he came there, he found that it had begun in a sailor's shed, and that, by the slightness of the buildings, and the awkwardness of the Chinese, it was getting head apace: but he perceived that, by pulling down some of the adjacent sheds, it might easily be extinguished; and particularly observing that it was running along a wooden cornice, which would soon communicate it to a great distance, he ordered his people to begin with tearing away that cornice; this was presently attempted, and would have been soon executed; but, in the meantime, he was told that, as there was no mandarin there to direct what was to be done, the Chinese would make him, the commodore, answerable for whatever should be pulled down by his orders. On this his people desisted; and he sent them to the English factory to assist in securing the Company's treasure and effects, as it was easy to foresee that no distance was a protection against the rage of such a fire, where so little was done to put a stop to it; for all this time the Chinese contented themselves with viewing it, and now and then holding one of their idols near it, which they seemed to expect should check its progress: however, at last, a mandarin came out of the city, attended by four or five hundred firemen: these made some feeble efforts to pull down the neighbouring houses; but by this time the fire had greatly extended itself, and was got amongst the merchants' warehouses; and the Chinese firemen, wanting both skill and spirit, were incapable of checking its violence; so that its fury increased upon them, and it was feared the whole city would be destroyed. In this general confusion the viceroy himself came thither, and the commodore was sent to, and was entreated to afford his assistance, being told that he might take any measure he should think most prudent in the present emergency. And now he went thither a second time, carrying with him about forty of his people; who, upon this occasion, exerted themselves in such a manner, as in that country was altogether without example: for they were rather animated than deterred by the flames and falling buildings among which they wrought; so that it was not uncommon to see the most forward of them tumble to the ground on the roofs, and amidst the ruins of houses, which their own efforts brought down with them. By their boldness and activity the fire was soon extinguished, to the amazement of the Chinese; and the buildings being all on one floor, the materials slight, the seamen, notwithstanding their daring behaviour, happily escaped with no other injuries than some considerable bruises.

The fire, though at last thus luckily extinguished, did great mischief during the time it continued; for it consumed a hundred shops and eleven streets full of warehouses, so that the damage amounted to an immense sum; and one of the Chinese merchants, well known to the English, whose name was Succoy, was supposed, for his own share, to have lost near two hundred thousand pounds sterling.   It raged indeed with unusual violence, for in many of the warehouses there were large quantities of camphor which greatly added to its fury, and produced a column of exceeding white flame, which shot up into the air to such a prodigious height, that the flame itself was plainly seen on board the Centurion, though she was thirty miles distant.

Whilst the commodore and his people were labouring at the fire, and the terror of its becoming general still possessed the whole city, several of the most considerable Chinese merchants came to Mr. Anson, to desire that he would let each of them have one of his soldiers (for such they styled his boat's crew from the uniformity of their dress) to guard their warehouses and dwelling-houses, which, from the known dishonesty of the populace, they feared would be pillaged in the tumult. Mr. Anson granted them this request; and all the men that he thus furnished to the Chinese behaved greatly to the satisfaction of their employers, who afterwards highly applauded their great diligence and fidelity.

By this means, the resolution of the English at the fire and their trustiness, and punctuality elsewhere, was the general subject of conversation amongst the Chinese: and the next morning, many of the principal inhabitants waited on the commodore to thank him for his assistance; frankly owning to him that they could never have extinguished the fire themselves, and that he had saved their city from being totally consumed. And soon after a message came to the commodore from the viceroy, appointing the 30th of November for his audience; which sudden resolution of the viceroy, in a matter that had been so long agitated in vain, was also owing to the signal service performed by Mr. Anson and his people at the fire, of which the viceroy himself had been in some measure an eye-witness.

The fixing this business of the audience was, on all accounts, a circumstance which Mr. Anson was much pleased with; as he was satisfied that the Chinese government would not have determined this point without having agreed among themselves to give up their pretensions to the duties they claimed, and to grant him all he could reasonably ask; for as they well knew the commodore's sentiments, it would have been a piece of imprudence, not consistent with the refined cunning of the Chinese, to have admitted him to an audience, only to have contested with him. And therefore, being himself perfectly easy about the result of his visit, he made all necessary preparations against the day; and engaged Mr. Flint, whom I have mentioned before, to act as interpreter in the conference; who, in this affair, as in all others, acquitted himself much to the commodore's satisfaction; repeating with great boldness, and doubtless with exactness, all that was given in charge, a part which no Chinese linguist would ever have performed with any tolerable fidelity.

At ten o'clock in the morning, on the day appointed, a mandarin came to the commodore to let him know that the viceroy was ready to receive him; on which the commodore and his retinue immediately set out: and as soon as he entered the outer gate of the city, he found a guard of two hundred soldiers drawn up ready to attend him; these conducted him to the great parade before the emperor's palace, where the viceroy then resided. In this parade, a body of troops, to the number of ten thousand, were drawn up under arms, and made a very fine appearance, being all of them new clothed for this ceremony: and Mr. Anson and his retinue having passed through the middle of them, he was then conducted to the great hall of audience, where he found the viceroy seated under a rich canopy in the emperor's chair of state, with all his council of mandarins attending: here there was a vacant seat prepared for the commodore, in which he was placed on his arrival: he was ranked the third in order from the viceroy, there being above him only the head of the law, and of the treasury, who in the Chinese government take place of all military officers. When the commodore was seated, he addressed himself to the viceroy by his interpreter, and began with reciting the various methods he had formerly taken to get an audience; adding, that he imputed the delays he had met with to the insincerity of those he had employed, and that he had therefore no other means left than to send, as he had done, his own officer with a letter to the gate. On the mention of this

the viceroy stopped the interpreter, and bade him assure
Mr. Anson that the first knowledge they had of his
being at Canton was from that letter.   Mr. Anson then
proceeded, and told him that the subjects of the King
of Great Britain trading to China had complained to
him, the commodore, of the vexatious impositions both
of the merchants and inferior custom-house officers, to
which they were frequently necessitated to submit, by
reason of the difficulty of getting access to the mandarins,
who alone could grant them redress: that it was his
(Mr. Anson's) duty, as an officer of the king of Great
Britain, to lay before the viceroy these grievances of the
British subjects, which he hoped the viceroy would take
into consideration, and would give orders, that for the
future there should be no just reason for complaint.
Here Mr. Anson paused, and waited some time in
expectation of an answer; but nothing being said, he
asked his interpreter if he was certain the viceroy understood what he had urged; the interpreter told him he
was certain it was understood, but he believed no reply
would be made to it.   Mr. Anson then represented to
the viceroy the case of the ship Hastingfield, which,
having been dismasted on the coast of China, had
arrived in the river of Canton but a few days before.   The
people on board this vessel had been great sufferers by
the fire; the captain in particular had all his goods
burnt, and lost besides, in the confusion, a chest of
treasure of four thousand five hundred tahel, which was
supposed to be stolen by the Chinese boatmen.   Mr.
Anson therefore desired that the captain might have the
assistance of the government, as it was apprehended the
money could never be recovered without the interposition

of the mandarins. And to this request the viceroy made answer, that in setting the emperor's customs for that ship, some abatement should be made in consideration of her losses.

And now the commodore having despatched the business with which the officers of the East India Company had entrusted him, he entered on his own affairs; acquainting the viceroy that the proper season was now set in for returning to Europe, and that he waited only for a license to ship off his provisions and stores, which were all ready; and that as soon as this should be granted him, and he should have gotten his necessaries on board, he intended to leave the river of. Canton, and to make the best of his way for England. The viceroy replied to this that the license should be immediately issued, and that everything should be ordered on board the following day. And finding that Mr. Anson had nothing further to insist on, the viceroy continued the conversation for some time, acknowledging in very civil terms how much the Chinese were obliged to him for his signal services at the fire, and owning that he had saved the city from being destroyed: and then observing that the Centurion had been a good while on their coast, he closed his discourse by wishing the commodore a good voyage to Europe. After which, the commodore, thanking him for his civility and assistance, took his leave.

As soon as the commodore was out of the hall of audience, he was much pressed to go into a neighbouring apartment, where there was an entertainment provided; but finding, on inquiry, that the. viceroy himself was not to be present, he declined the invitation, and departed, attended in the same manner as at his arrival; only at his leaving the city he was saluted by three guns, which are as many as in that country are ever fired on any ceremony. Thus the commodore, to his great joy, at last finished this troublesome affair, which, for the preceding four months, had given him great disquietude. Indeed he was highly pleased with procuring a license for the shipping of his stores and provisions; for thereby he was enabled to return to Great Britain with the first of the monsoon, and to prevent all intelligence of his being expected: but this, though a very important point, was not the circumstance which gave him the greatest satisfaction; for he was more particularly attentive to the authentic precedent established on this occcasion, by which His Majesty's ships of war are for the future exempted from all demands of duty in any of the ports of China.

In pursuance of the promises of the viceroy, the provisions were begun to be sent on board the day after the audience; and, four days after, the commodore embarked at Canton for the Centurion; and, on the 7th of December. the Centurion and her prize unmoored, and stood down the river, passing through the Bocca Tigris on the 10th. And on this occasion I must observe that the Chinese had taken care to man the two forts, on each side of that passage, with as many men as they could well contain, the greatest part of them armed with pikes and matchlock muskets. These garrisons affected to show themselves as much as possible to the ships, and were doubtless intended to induce Mr. Anson to think more reverently than he had hitherto done of the Chinese military power: for this purpose they were equipped with much parade, having a great number of colours exposed to view; and on the castle in particular there were laid considerable heaps of large stones; and a soldier of unusual size, dressed in very sightly armour, stalked about on the parapet with a battle axe in his hand, endeavouring to put on as important and martial an air as possible, though some of the observers on board the Centurion shrewdly suspected, from the appearance of his armour, that instead of steel, it was composed only of a particular kind of glittering paper.

But it is time to return to the commodore, whom I left with his two ships without the Bocca Tigris; and who, on the 12th of December, anchored before the town of Macao.

Whilst the ships lay here, the merchants of Macao finished their agreement for the galleon, for which they had offered 6000 dollars; this was much short of her value, but the impatience of the commodore to get to sea, to which the merchants were no strangers, prompted them to insist on so unequal a bargain. Mr. Anson had learnt enough from the English at Canton to conjecture that the war betwixt Great Britain and Spain was still continued; and that probably the French might engage in the assistance of Spain before he could arrive in Great Britain; and, therefore, knowing that no intelligence could get to Europe of the prize he had taken, and the treasure he had on board, till the return of the merchantmen from Canton, he was resolved to make all possible expedition in getting back, that he might be himself the first messenger of his own good fortune, and might thereby prevent the enemy from forming any projects to intercept him: for these reasons, he, to avoid all delay, accepted of the sum offered for the galleon; and she being delivered to the merchants, the 15th of December 1743, the Centurion, the same day, got under sail, on her return to England. And, on the 3rd of January, she came to an anchor at Prince's Island in the Straits of Sunda, and continued there wooding and watering till the 8th; when she weighed and stood for the Cape of Good Hope, where, on the 11th of March, she anchored in Table Bay.

The Cape of Good Hope is situated in a temperate climate, where the excesses of heat and cold are rarely known; and the Dutch inhabitants, who are numerous, and who here retain their native industry, have stocked it with prodigious plenty of all sorts of fruits and provisions; most of which, either from the equality of the seasons, or the peculiarity of the soil, are more delicious in their kind than can be met with elsewhere: so that by these, and by the excellent water which abounds there, this settlement is the best provided of any in the known world, for the refreshment of seamen after long voyages. Here the commodore continued till the beginning of April, highly delighted with the place, which by its extraordinary accommodations, the healthiness of its air, and the picturesque appearance of the country, all enlivened by the addition of a civilised colony, was not disgraced in an imaginary comparison with the valleys of Juan Fernandes, and the lawns of Tinian. During his stay he entered about forty new men; and having, by the 3rd of April 1744, completed his water and provision, he, on that day, weighed and put to sea; and, the 19th of the same month, they saw the island of St. Helena, which however they did not touch at, but stood on their

way; and, on the 10th of June, being then in soundings,
they spoke with an English ship from Amsterdam bound
for Philadelphia, whence they received the first intelligence of a French war; the twelfth, they got sight of the
Lizard; and the fifteenth, in the evening, to their infinite
joy, they came safe to an anchor at Spithead.   But that
the signal perils, which had so often threatened them in
the preceding part of the enterprise, might pursue them
to the very last, Mr. Anson learnt, on his arrival, that
there was a French fleet of considerable force cruising
in the chops of the Channel; which, by the account of
their position, he found the Centurion had run through,
and had been all the time concealed by a fog.   Thus
was this expedition finished, when it had lasted three
years and nine months; after having, by its event,
strongly evinced this important truth, that though
prudence, intrepidity, and perseverance united, are not
exempted from the blows of adverse fortune;
yet in a long series of transactions, they
usually rise superior to its power,
and in the end rarely fail of
proving successful.

BINDING SECT. MAY 1 6 1966

DA
87
.1
A6A3
1905

Anson, George Anson, baron
The taking of the galleon

PLEASE DO NOT REMOVE

CARDS OR SLIPS FROM THIS POCKET

UNIVERSITY OF TORONTO LIBRARY